MW00560091

SPSS® 7.5 for Windows® Brief Guide

SPSS Inc.

SPSS Inc.
444 N. Michigan Avenue
Chicago, Illinois 60611
Tel: (312) 329-2400
Fax: (312) 329-3668

SPSS Federal Systems (U.S.)
SPSS Argentina srl
SPSS Asia Pacific Pte. Ltd.
SPSS Australasia Pty. Ltd.
SPSS Belgium
SPSS Benelux BV
SPSS Central and Eastern Europe
SPSS East Mediterranea and Africa
SPSS France SARL
SPSS Germany
SPSS Hellas SA
SPSS Hispanoportuguesa S.L.
SPSS Ireland
SPSS Israel Ltd.
SPSS Italia srl
SPSS Japan Inc.
SPSS Korea
SPSS Latin America
SPSS Malaysia Sdn Bhd
SPSS Mexico SA de CV
SPSS Middle East and South Asia
SPSS Scandinavia AB
SPSS Schweiz AG
SPSS Singapore Pte. Ltd.
SPSS Taiwan Corp.
SPSS UK Ltd.

For more information about SPSS® software products, please visit our WWW site at *http://www.spss.com* or contact

Marketing Department
SPSS Inc.
444 North Michigan Avenue
Chicago, IL 60611
Tel: (312) 329-2400
Fax: (312) 329-3668

SPSS® 7.5 for Windows® Brief Guide
Copyright © 1997 by SPSS Inc.
 Published by Prentice-Hall, Inc.
Simon & Schuster / A Viacom Company
Upper Saddle River, New Jersey

Printed in the United States of America.

4 5 6 7 8 9 0   03 02 01 00 99 98 97

ISBN 0-13-656885-8

Preface

SPSS for Windows

SPSS 7.5 is a comprehensive system for analyzing data. SPSS can take data from almost any type of file and use them to generate tabulated reports, charts and plots of distributions and trends, descriptive statistics, and complex statistical analyses.

SPSS makes statistical analysis more accessible for the beginner and more convenient for the experienced user. Simple menus and dialog box selections make it possible to perform complex analyses without typing a single line of command syntax. The Data Editor offers a simple and efficient spreadsheet-like facility for entering data and browsing the working data file. High-resolution, presentation-quality charts and plots are included as part of the Base and Student Version systems.

The *SPSS 7.5 for Windows Brief Guide* provides a set of tutorials designed to acquaint you with the various components of the SPSS system. You can work through the tutorials in sequence or turn to the topics for which you need additional information. You can use this book as a supplement to the online tutorial that is included with the SPSS 7.5 system or ignore the online tutorial and start with the tutorials found here.

Internet Resources

The SPSS home page on the World Wide Web offers answers to frequently asked questions about installing and running SPSS software, access to the SPSS newsletter *Keywords*, data files, and other useful information. The URL (address) for the SPSS home page is *http://www.spss.com*.

In addition, the SPSS USENET discussion group (not sponsored by SPSS) is open to anyone interested in SPSS products. The USENET address is *comp.soft-sys.stat.spss*. It deals with computer, statistical, and other operational issues related to SPSS software.

You can also subscribe to an E-mail message list that is gatewayed to the USENET group. To subscribe, send an E-mail message to *listserv@uga.cc.uga.edu*. The text of the E-mail message should be: subscribe SPSSX-L firstname lastname. You can then post messages to the list by sending an E-mail message to *SPSSX-L@uga.cc.uga.edu*.

Sample Data

The data used for all but one example in this book are from a file named *Employee data.sav*. This file is included with SPSS 7.5 for Windows and the Student Version. The time series example uses a file named *Inventor.sav*. This file is included only with the Student Version.

These files are also available through the following methods:

SPSS WWW site. You can download the files from the SPSS home page at *http://www.spss.com/Support*. Look for the link to Datasets under Ftp Archives.

Anonymous FTP. The files are also available via anonymous FTP at *ftp.spss.com*. The location is *\pub\spss\sample\datasets* and the filename is *75brief.exe*.

Additional Publications

The *SPSS 7.5 Guide to Data Analysis* introduces the concepts of data analysis, from collecting and coding data to interpreting the results of statistical analyses. The guide is appropriate for students and professionals, and includes instructions for operating SPSS 7.5 for Windows and the Student Version.

For additional information about the features and operations of SPSS Base 7.5, you can consult the *SPSS Base 7.5 for Windows User's Guide*. A companion guide, *SPSS Base 7.5 Applications Guide*, provides examples of statistical procedures found in SPSS Base 7.5.

In addition, beneath the menus and dialog boxes, SPSS uses a command language. Some extended features of the system can be accessed only via command syntax. (Those features are not available in the Student Version.) Complete command syntax is documented in the *SPSS Base 7.5 Syntax Reference Guide*.

The complete title and ISBN for each of these publications are listed below:

- *SPSS 7.5 Guide to Data Analysis* ISBN 0-13-656877-7
- *SPSS Base 7.5 for Windows User's Guide* ISBN 0-13-657214-6
- *SPSS Base 7.5 Applications Guide* ISBN 0-13-656992-7
- *SPSS Base 7.5 Syntax Reference Guide* ISBN 0-13-656943-9

Individuals in the United States can order these manuals by calling Prentice Hall at 1-800-947-7700. If you represent a bookstore or have a Prentice Hall account, call 1-800-382-3419. In Canada, call 1-800-567-3800. Outside of North America, contact your local Prentice Hall office.

Individuals worldwide can also order manuals directly from the SPSS WWW site at *http://www.spss.com/Pubs*. For telephone orders in the United States and Canada, call SPSS Inc. at 1-800-253-2565. For telephone orders outside of North America, contact your local SPSS office, listed on p. ix.

SPSS Options

The following options are available as add-on enhancements to the full (not Student Version) SPSS Base system:

SPSS Professional Statistics™ provides more advanced regression techniques, including weighted and two-stage least-squares, logistic regression, and nonlinear regression, plus multidimensional scaling and reliability analysis.

SPSS Advanced Statistics™ includes sophisticated techniques such as general linear models, variance component analysis, loglinear and probit analysis, Cox regression, and Kaplan-Meier and actuarial survival analysis.

SPSS Exact Tests™ calculates exact *p* values for statistical tests when small or very unevenly distributed samples could make the usual tests inaccurate.

SPSS Tables™ creates a variety of presentation-quality tabular reports, including complex stub-and-banner tables and displays of multiple response data.

SPSS Trends™ performs comprehensive forecasting and time series analyses with multiple curve-fitting models, smoothing models, and methods for estimating autoregressive functions.

SPSS Categories® performs conjoint analysis and optimal scaling procedures, including correspondence analysis.

SPSS CHAID™ simplifies tabular analysis of categorical data, develops predictive models, screens out extraneous predictor variables, and produces easy-to-read tree diagrams that segment a population into subgroups that share similar characteristics.

AMOS performs powerful structural equation modeling and confirmatory factor analysis through an easy-to-use interface.

Neural Connection™ provides state-of-the-art neural network power and flexibility for prediction, classification, time series analysis, and data segmentation.

MapInfo® creates thematic maps for data visualization. Choose geographic regions from country to street level or create your own boundary files.

allCLEAR™ III is a full-featured flowchart program. Create diagrams for causes and effects, process flow, network and deployment; build decision trees, organizational charts, and procedural charts.

Training Seminars

SPSS Inc. provides both public and onsite training seminars for SPSS. All seminars feature hands-on workshops. SPSS seminars will be offered in major U.S. and European cities on a regular basis. For more information on these seminars, call your local office, listed on p. ix.

Technical Support

The services of SPSS Technical Support are available to registered customers of SPSS. (Student Version customers should read the special section on technical support on p. vii.) Customers may contact Technical Support for assistance in using SPSS products or for installation help for one of the supported hardware environments. To reach Technical Support, see the SPSS home page on the World Wide Web at *http://www.spss.com*, or call your local office, listed on p. ix. Be prepared to identify yourself, your organization, and the serial number of your system.

Tell Us Your Thoughts

Your comments are important. Please send us a letter and let us know about your experiences with SPSS products. We especially like to hear about new and interesting applications using the SPSS system. Write to SPSS Inc. Marketing Department, Attn: Director of Product Planning, 444 N. Michigan Avenue, Chicago IL, 60611.

SPSS for Windows Student Version

Capability

SPSS 7.5 for Windows Student Version is a limited but still powerful version of SPSS for Windows. The Student Version contains all of the important data analysis tools contained in the full SPSS Base system, including:

- Spreadsheet-like Data Editor for entering, modifying, and viewing data files.
- Statistical procedures including *t* tests, analysis of variance, crosstabulations, and multiple regression.
- High-resolution graphics for an extensive array of analytical and presentation charts and tables.

Limitations

Created for classroom instruction, the use of the Student Version is limited to students and instructors for educational purposes only. The Student Version does not contain all of the functions of SPSS 7.5 for Windows. The following limitations apply to SPSS 7.5 for Windows Student Version:

- Data files cannot contain more than 50 variables.
- Data files cannot contain more than 1500 cases.
- SPSS add-on modules (such as Professional or Advanced Statistics) cannot be used with the Student Version.
- SPSS command syntax is not available to the user. This means that it is not possible to repeat an analysis by saving a series of commands in a syntax or "job" file, as can be done in the full version of SPSS.
- Scripting and automation are not available to the user. This means that you cannot create scripts that automate tasks that you repeat often, as can be done in the full version of SPSS.

Customer Service

To report any damaged or missing components of your SPSS 7.5 for Windows Student Version, call Prentice Hall Customer Service at 1-800-922-0579 (1-800-567-3800 in Canada). Outside of the United States, contact your local Prentice Hall representative.

Technical Support for Students

Students should obtain technical support from their instructors or from local support staff identified by their instructors. Technical support from SPSS for SPSS 7.5 for Windows Student Version is provided *only to instructors using the system for classroom instruction.*

Before seeking assistance from your instructor, please write down the information described below. Without this information, your instructor may be unable to assist you:

- The type of PC you are using, as well as the amount of RAM and free disk space you have.
- The operating system of your PC.
- A clear description of what happened and what you were doing when the problem occurred. If possible, please try to reproduce the problem with one of the sample data files provided with the program.
- The exact wording of any error or warning messages that appeared on your screen.
- How you tried to solve the problem on your own.

Technical Support for Instructors

Instructors using the Student Version for classroom instruction may contact SPSS Technical Support for assistance. In the United States and Canada, call SPSS Technical Support at 1-312-329-3410, or send an E-mail to *support@spss.com*. Please include your name, title, and academic institution.

Instructors outside of the United States and Canada should contact your local SPSS office through the SPSS home page at *http://www.spss.com*, or call your local office, listed on p. ix.

Contacting SPSS Inc.

If you would like to be on our mailing list, contact one of our offices below. We will send you a copy of our newsletter and let you know about SPSS Inc. activities in your area.

SPSS Inc.
Chicago, Illinois, U.S.A.
Tel: 1.312.329.2400
Fax: 1.312.329.3668
Customer Service:
1.800.521.1337
Sales:
1.800.543.2185
sales@spss.com
Training:
1.800.543.6607
Technical Support:
1.312.329.3410
support@spss.com

SPSS Federal Systems
Arlington, Virginia, U.S.A.
Tel: 1.703.527.6777
Fax: 1.703.527.6866

SPSS Argentina srl
Buenos Aires, Argentina
Tel: +541.816.4086
Fax: +541.814.5030

SPSS Asia Pacific Pte. Ltd.
Singapore, Singapore
Tel: +65.3922.738
Fax: +65.3922.739

SPSS Australasia Pty. Ltd.
Sydney, Australia
Tel: +61.2.9954.5660
Fax: +61.2.9954.5616

SPSS Belgium
Heverlee, Belgium
Tel: +32.162.389.82
Fax: +32.1620.0888

SPSS Benelux BV
Gorinchem, The Netherlands
Tel: +31.183.636711
Fax: +31.183.635839

**SPSS Central and
Eastern Europe**
Woking, Surrey, U.K.
Tel: +44.(0)1483.719200
Fax: +44.(0)1483.719290

SPSS East Mediterranea and Africa
Herzlia, Israel
Tel: +972.9.526700
Fax: +972.9.526715

SPSS France SARL
Boulogne, France
Tel: +33.1.4699.9670
Fax: +33.1.4684.0180

SPSS Germany
Munich, Germany
Tel: +49.89.4890740
Fax: +49.89.4483115

SPSS Hellas SA
Athens, Greece
Tel: +30.1.7251925
Fax: +30.1.7249124

SPSS Hispanoportuguesa S.L.
Madrid, Spain
Tel: +34.91.447.3700
Fax: +34.91.448.6692

SPSS Ireland
Dublin, Ireland
Tel: +353.1.66.13788
Fax: +353.1.661.5200

SPSS Israel Ltd.
Herzlia, Israel
Tel: +972.9.526700
Fax: +972.9.526715

SPSS Italia srl
Bologna, Italy
Tel: +39.51.252573
Fax: +39.51.253285

SPSS Japan Inc.
Tokyo, Japan
Tel: +81.3.5466.5511
Fax: +81.3.5466.5621

SPSS Korea
Seoul, Korea
Tel: +82.2.552.9415
Fax: +82.2.539.0136

SPSS Latin America
Chicago, Illinois, U.S.A.
Tel: 1.312.494.3226
Fax: 1.312. 494.3227

SPSS Malaysia Sdn Bhd
Selangor, Malaysia
Tel: +603.704.5877
Fax: +603.704.5790

SPSS Mexico SA de CV
Mexico DF, Mexico
Tel: +52.5.575.3091
Fax: +52.5.575.2527

**SPSS Middle East and
South Asia**
Dubai, UAE
Tel: +971.4.525536
Fax: +971.4.524669

SPSS Newton
Newton, Massachusetts
Tel: 1.617.965.6755
Fax: 1.617.965.5310

SPSS Scandinavia AB
Stockholm, Sweden
Tel: +46.8.102610
Fax: +46.8.102550

SPSS Schweiz AG
Zurich, Switzerland
Tel: +41.1.201.0930
Fax: +41.1.201.0921

SPSS Singapore Pte. Ltd.
Singapore, Singapore
Tel: +65.2991238
Fax: +65.2990849

SPSS Taiwan Corp.
Taipei, Republic of China
Tel: +886.2.5771100
Fax: +886.2.5701717

SPSS UK Ltd.
Woking, Surrey, U.K.
Tel: +44.1483.719200
Fax: +44.1483.719290

Contents

1

A Quick Tour

This tour provides a quick preview of SPSS for Windows. More detailed information is available in later chapters and in the online Help system. The following techniques are briefly demonstrated:

- Starting and exiting from SPSS
- Opening a data file in the SPSS Data Editor
- Using the SPSS Statistics menu to obtain a frequency table and bar chart
- Viewing output
- Getting information from online Help and the online tutorial

This session will use the mouse. If you need information about using Windows or the mouse, see your Windows documentation.

The Online Tutorial

The SPSS online tutorial, which is part of the SPSS Help that is installed with the SPSS for Windows software, provides an overview of SPSS. While the online tutorial lacks the "hands-on" approach of the tutorials in this manual, it provides a more complete introduction to a number of SPSS features, such as the toolbar. (Other topics, such as data transformations, are covered more extensively in the manual.)

The tutorial can be accessed from any SPSS window. (See "Getting Started" on p. 2 for details on starting SPSS.) To start the tutorial, choose Tutorial from the Help menu in any SPSS window. This opens the Contents tab, as shown in Figure 1.1.

Figure 1.1   Help Topics: online Tutorial

If SPSS is already running, you can run the tutorial by choosing Tutorial from the Help menu.

The Contents tab is organized by topic, like a table of contents. Double-click on items with a book icon to expand or collapse the contents. Double-click on an item to go to that help topic.

Getting Started

To start an SPSS session:

❶ Choose SPSS 7.5 for Windows or SPSS 7.5 for Windows Student Version from the Programs submenu on the Windows Start menu.

Figure 1.2   Starting SPSS

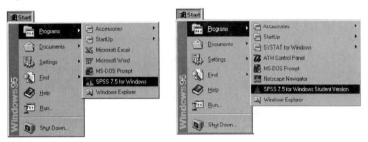

This opens the SPSS Data Editor window, as shown in Figure 1.3.

Figure 1.3   SPSS Data Editor window

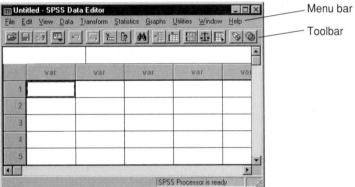

Opening a Data File

For this example, the data are in a file named *Employee data.sav*. (See the Preface if you don't find this file on your system or Chapter 4 if you need more information about opening a data file.)

❶ Click File on the menu bar.

This opens the File menu, which contains a list of options (New, Open, etc.).

❷ Click Open....

This opens the Open File dialog box, as shown in Figure 1.4.

Figure 1.4   Opening a previously saved data file

List of files

File name box

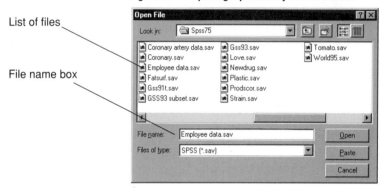

❸ Select *Employee data.sav* on the list.

This enters the name of the file in the File name box.

Another way to open a file is to double-click on the filename on the list.

❹ Click Open.

This opens the data file. The Data Editor window, containing data from *Employee data.sav*, is shown in Figure 1.5.

Figure 1.5   Data Editor window

Cases

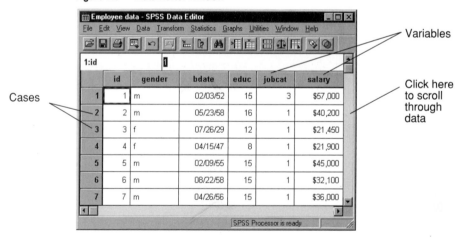

Variables

Click here to scroll through data

Some variables use numeric codes for categories. For the variable minority, 0 is a code for "no" and 1 is a code for "yes."

At the top of the data window is a row of names for the types of information included in the columns of the data file. These are called **variables**. The first variable, *id*, indicates that the numbers in the first column represent ID numbers for employees. Five columns to the right, the variable *salary* indicates that the column contains the annual salary for each employee.

The rows in the data file are called **cases**. In this file, each of 474 cases contains the data for one employee.

Calculating Simple Statistics

Now that you have a data file open in SPSS, you can calculate some simple statistics. When you first start to analyze a set of data, you often want to know how many cases are in various categories. SPSS does the counting for you and displays the results in a table.

To see the names of the job categories, you can double-click on the variable jobcat at the top of the column and then click Labels....

The variable *jobcat* contains codes for employee job categories. Each type of job is coded with a number between 1 and 3. A label for each of the code numbers is stored in the data file, and SPSS will use the labels when it displays the results.

❶ To calculate how many cases are in specified categories, from the menus choose:

Statistics
  Summarize ▶
    Frequencies...

Figure 1.6 shows the Statistics menu and Summarize submenu.

Figure 1.6   Choosing a statistical procedure

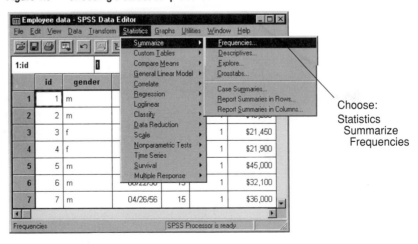

Choose:
Statistics
  Summarize
    Frequencies

Choosing the Frequencies procedure from the menus opens the Frequencies dialog box, as shown in Figure 1.7. The Frequencies procedure counts the number of cases in various categories

Figure 1.7   Selecting variables

Click here
to move jobcat

List of available
variables

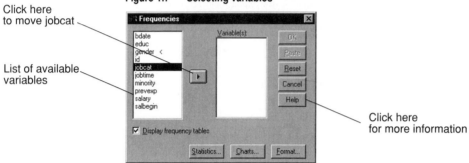

Click here
for more information

The variables available in the *Employee data.sav* data file are listed in the box on the left.

You can double-click on jobcat to move it to the Variable(s) list.

❷ Select *jobcat* and then click ▶.

This moves *jobcat* to the Variable(s) list. At this point, look at the SPSS Help facility for information about what to do next. When you are learning something new in SPSS, press Help whenever you need assistance.

❸ Click Help in the dialog box.

This opens a window containing information about the current dialog box, Frequencies, as shown in Figure 1.8.

Figure 1.8   Frequencies Help

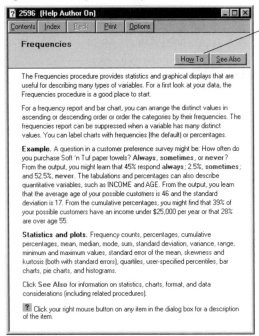

Click here to find out how to use the dialog box to run the procedure

❹ To exit from the Help window, click the Close box in the upper right corner of the Help window.

This returns you to the Frequencies dialog box.

❺ Click Charts... to open the Frequencies Charts dialog box, as shown in Figure 1.9.

Figure 1.9   Selecting a chart type

Click here

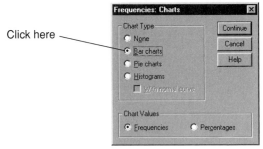

⑥ Select Bar charts.

⑦ Click Continue.

This closes the Frequencies Charts dialog box.

⑧ In the Frequencies dialog box, click OK.

The results are displayed in the Output Navigator window.

Figure 1.10   Output Navigator

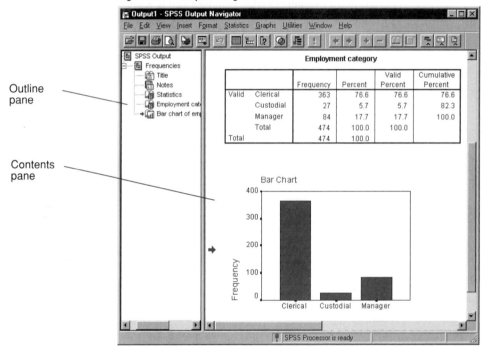

Viewing the Output

The Output Navigator contains an outline pane and a contents pane. You can view different parts of your output by using the scrollbars in the contents pane or by clicking the item you want to view in the outline pane.

Experimenting

If you want to try some other procedures, go ahead and experiment now. For example, you could try opening the Statistics menu and selecting Summarize ▶ and Descriptives... to display summary statistics and calculate standardized values. After the dialog box opens, select the variables *salbegin* and *salary*.

If you aren't sure how the descriptive statistics are defined, click Options in the Descriptives dialog box. Then, click your right mouse button on any statistic you don't recognize and a definition will pop up.

Click OK in the Descriptives dialog box to run the Descriptives procedure.

Ending the SPSS Session

❶ To exit from SPSS, from the menus choose:

File
  Exit SPSS

as shown in Figure 1.11.

Figure 1.11   Exiting SPSS

Click here to end
the SPSS session

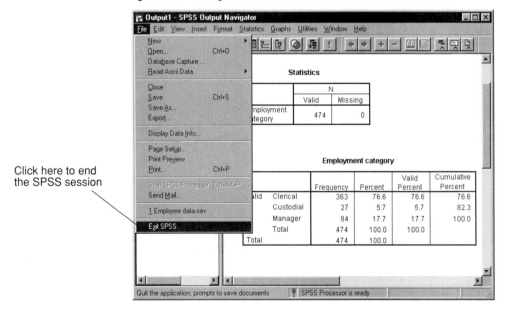

SPSS asks if you want to save the contents of the Output Navigator.

❷ Click No.

This ends the SPSS session.

Should I Save the Data File?

If SPSS asks if you want to save the data file, click **No**. This will happen only if you changed something in the data file, such as a data value, a variable name, or the order of the cases. When you use a file and see it in the Data Editor, the actual copy on the disk is not changed. The disk file is changed only if you save the file. Since the *Employee data.sav* file will be used in its original form in the next few chapters, it should not be changed.

What's Next?

The tutorials in the following chapters allow you to explore SPSS in greater depth, continuing the hands-on approach used in this quick tour. In addition, brief information on the basics of running selected statistical procedures is presented in the last section of this book. For detailed information on statistical procedures, consult a statistics or data analysis textbook.

The SPSS online tutorial provides a more complete introduction to a number of SPSS features such as the toolbar. (See "The Online Tutorial" on p. 1.)

For the most complete coverage of SPSS, consult the online Help system. Chapter 2 provides an introduction to Help.

2 Tutorial: Using the Help System

The SPSS for Windows Help provides the information that you need to use SPSS and understand the results. This tutorial demonstrates the following:

- Locating topics in the Help contents
- Searching the Help index for a specified topic

This tutorial can be done with any open data file (such as *Employee data.sav*), or it can be done with the Data Editor empty.

Locating Topics in the Help Contents

Suppose that you want to make a chart of your data. You have a picture in mind of what the chart should look like, but you are unsure of what it is called or whether it is available in SPSS. To find out, you can consult the Help system, as illustrated in the following steps:

You can also access Help by clicking on the Help button in any dialog box. Information about that dialog box will automatically be displayed.

1 From the menus choose:

Help
  Topics

2 Click the Contents tab.

This opens the Help Contents window, as shown in Figure 2.1. (You can always return to this window from anywhere in SPSS Help by selecting the Contents button near the top of the Help window.)

Figure 2.1   Help system Contents tab

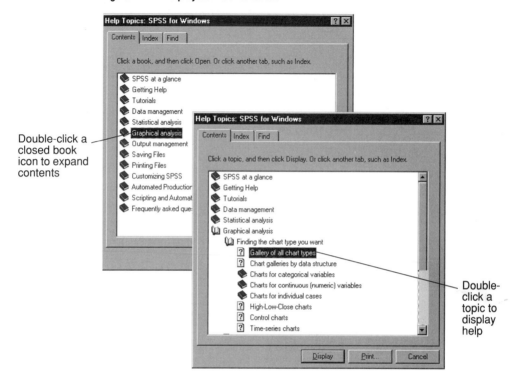

Double-click a
closed book
icon to expand
contents

Double-
click a
topic to
display
help

③ Double-click the closed book icon for Graphical analysis.

④ Double-click the closed book icon for Finding the chart type you want.

Double-clicking book icons in the Contents tab expands and collapses the
displayed list of topics.

⑤ Double-click the topic Gallery of all chart types.

This takes you to a window displaying icons for all of the chart types available
in SPSS for Windows (see Figure 2.2).

Figure 2.2   Charts available in SPSS

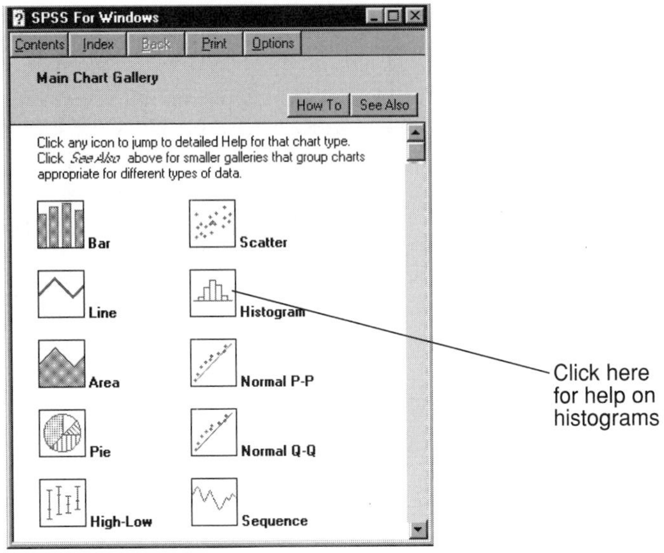

Highlighted text and icons indicate "jumps" or "pop-ups." When you see the hand icon

you can click for more information.

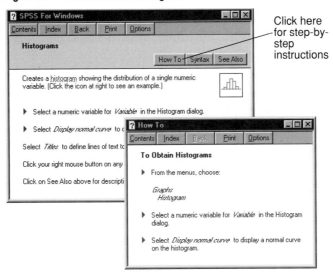

6 Click on the histogram icon, as shown in Figure 2.2.

This jumps you to a topic that describes the Histograms dialog box, as shown in Figure 2.3.

Figure 2.3   Information on histograms

After reading the topic, if you decide to create a histogram, you need to know how to open the Histograms dialog box.

❼ Click the How To button in the Help window, as shown in Figure 2.3.

Another Help window displays instructions on how to open the Histograms dialog box. When you have finished reading the information, close the Help windows. Another way to access Help is illustrated in the next section.

Searching

Rather than using the Help Contents tab, you can often find the information you want more quickly by using Help's search feature. For example, suppose that you want to find out how to calculate percentiles and you do not find percentiles on the statistics menus.

❶ From the SPSS menus choose:

Help
  Topics

❷ Click the Index tab.

Figure 2.4   Help Index tab

Another way to open the Index tab box is to click on the Index button in the Help window.

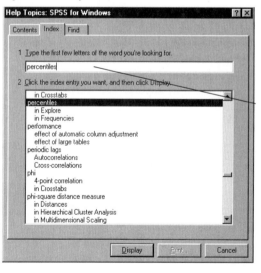

Type percentiles

The window opens with the cursor in the text box.

❸ Type **percentiles** in the text box.

The list scrolls until Percentiles is highlighted.

Several topics are listed under Percentiles.

④ Double-click the topic labeled in Frequencies.

This opens a Help window that gives you information about statistics available for the Frequencies procedure, as shown in Figure 2.5.

Figure 2.5   Information about Frequencies statistics

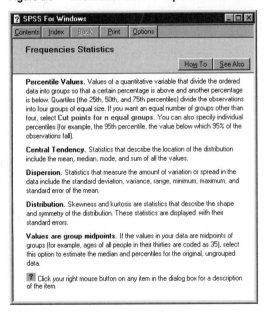

How to Ask for Help

You can ask for help in any of the following ways:

Click on the Help button in any dialog box for information about that dialog box.

- Click on the Help button in any dialog box for information about that dialog box.
- From the SPSS menu bar, open the Help menu and select a topic.
- Click your right mouse button on any control in a dialog box for a pop-up explanation of what the control does.
- Click your right mouse button on a label in an activated pivot table and select "What's This" from the context menu for a pop-up definition of the term.

Figure 2.6   Pop-up definitions with right mouse button

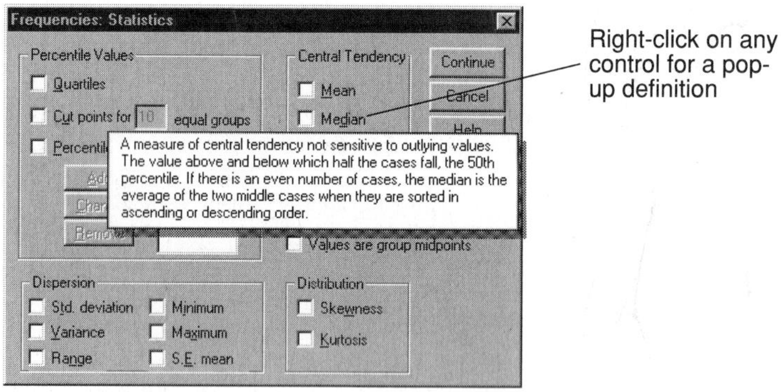

Right-click on any control for a pop-up definition

What's Next?

At this point, you can exit SPSS. If you exit from SPSS and you have changed the data file in any way, you will be asked whether you want to save the changes. *Do not* save changes to the *Employee data.sav* data file.

If you want to try some more statistics, brief tutorials for selected procedures are provided in Chapter 12.

3 Tutorial: Using the Data Editor

This tutorial introduces the use of the Data Editor and demonstrates the following:

- Entering data in the Data Editor
- Naming variables
- Defining a string variable
- Defining value labels for a variable
- Saving data files

When you start an SPSS session, SPSS automatically opens the Data Editor window, as shown in Figure 3.1. (See Chapter 1 if you do not know how to start SPSS.)

Figure 3.1   SPSS Data Editor

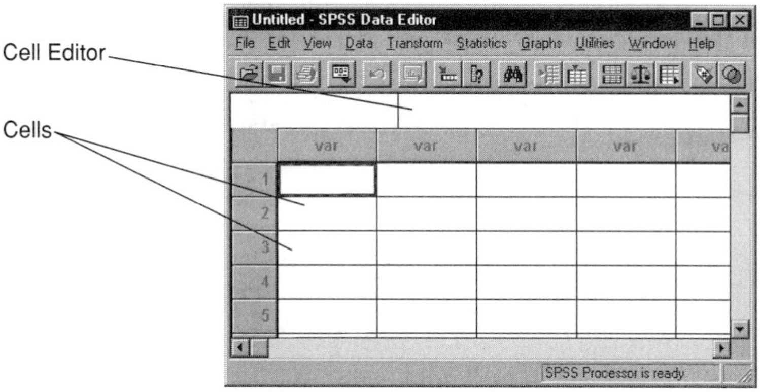

The Data Editor provides a convenient spreadsheet-like facility for entering, editing, and displaying the contents of your data file. You can use the Data Editor to enter data and create a data file. If you open a previously saved data file, you can use the Data Editor to change data values and add or delete cases and variables.

Entering Data

Entering numeric data (numbers) in the Data Editor is easy. You simply type the number in the appropriate cell and press ⏎Enter. For example, you could enter the age for the students in your class:

❶ Click on the first cell in the Data Editor (top left corner) and type:

21

The number appears in the cell editor at the top of the Data Editor as you enter it but is not displayed in the cell until you press ⏎Enter.

By entering data in the cell, you automatically create a variable, and SPSS gives it the default name *var00001*, which is displayed at the top of the column. (Replacing default variable names is discussed on p. 19. Variable naming rules are listed on p. 24.)

❷ Continue entering values in the first column:

19 ⏎Enter

22 ⏎Enter

⬇ (skip this cell; do not enter a value)

22 ⏎Enter

20 ⏎Enter

19 ⏎Enter

The Data Editor should now look like Figure 3.2.

Figure 3.2   Data Editor after entering data

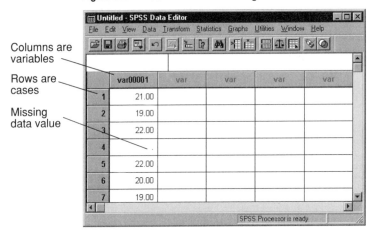

Columns are variables

Rows are cases

Missing data value

A period is displayed in the cell that does not have a data value. The period represents the **system-missing value**. In this example, it could be a person in the class who did not want to reveal his or her age.

Naming Variables

The variable names NewVar, newvar, and NEWVAR are all identical in SPSS.

To replace the default variable name with a more descriptive variable name:

❶ Double-click the variable name *var00001* at the top of the first column in the Data Editor window, or select any cell in the first column and from the menus choose:

Data
  Define Variable...

This opens the Define Variable dialog box.

❷ Delete the default variable name *var00001* and type **age** in the Variable Name text box.

❸ Click OK.

This closes the Define Variable dialog box and changes the variable name to *age*, which is now displayed at the top of the first column in the Data Editor.

Defining Variables

Names, dates, and other non-numeric data must be defined before you can enter them. If you want to enter anything other than simple numbers, you need to tell SPSS what kind of non-numeric data you want to enter. With SPSS, you can also assign descriptive variable labels and value labels that make it easier to interpret your data, charts, and statistical results.

❶ Click on the first cell in the second column of the Data Editor (to the right of the column of numbers you entered earlier).

❷ Type **m** (or any other letter).

SPSS does not accept the value, and your computer probably beeps at you. Since "m" is not a numeric value, you need to define the data type for SPSS before you can enter the value.

❸ Double-click on the top of the second column (on the dimmed heading labeled var), or click any cell in the second column, and from the menus choose:

Data
  Define Variable...

This opens the Define Variable dialog box, as shown in Figure 3.3.

Figure 3.3   Define Variable dialog box

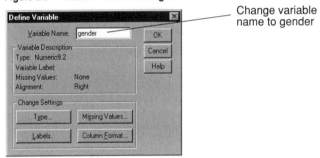

Change variable
name to gender

④ Delete the default variable name *var00002* and type **gender** in the Variable Name text box.

⑤ Click Type... in the Change Settings group.

This opens the Define Variable Type dialog box, as shown in Figure 3.4.

Figure 3.4   Define Variable Type dialog box

Select
String

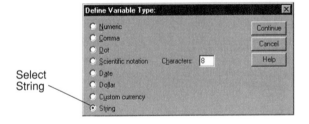

⑥ Select String and then click Continue to return to the Define Variable dialog box.

SPSS now knows that the variable *gender* is a string variable. A **string variable** can contain both letters and numbers.

⑦ Click Labels... in the Change Settings group at the bottom of the Define Variable dialog box.

This opens the Define Labels dialog box, as shown in Figure 3.5.

Figure 3.5   Define Labels dialog box

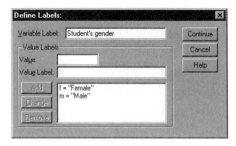

⑧ Type **Student's gender** in the Variable Label text box.

This descriptive variable label will be displayed in statistical output and in charts that use the variable *gender*.

⑨ Type **m** in the Value text box.

⑩ Type **Male** in the Value Label text box.

⑪ Click Add.

⑫ Go back and type **f** in the Value text box.

⑬ Type **Female** in the Value Label text box.

⑭ Click Add, and then click Continue to return to the Define Variable dialog box.

⑮ Click OK to accept the variable definition and close the Define Variable dialog box.

String data values are case sensitive. A value label assigned to m will not be used for data entered as M.

You can now use the single letter codes **m** and **f** (lowercase in this example) for data entry, and SPSS will display the more descriptive value labels, *Male* and *Female*, in statistical output and charts.

⑯ In the Data Editor column for the string variable *gender*, type the following:

m ⏎Enter

m ⏎Enter

f ⏎Enter

m ⏎Enter

f ⏎Enter

f ⏎Enter

m ⏎Enter

You can also display value labels by clicking

⑰ From the menus choose:

> View
>   Value Labels

The value labels for *gender* are now displayed in the Data Editor, as shown in Figure 3.6. If you click on any cell in the column for the variable *gender*, the actual value will be displayed in the cell editor at the top of the Data Editor window.

Figure 3.6   Data Editor with value labels displayed

You can open a window summarizing variable definition information by clicking

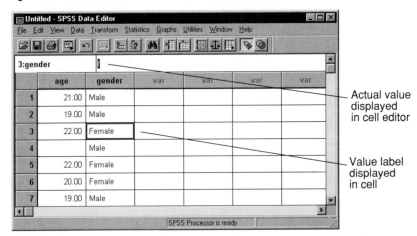

Saving a Data File

If you want to save the data file:

1. Make the Data Editor the active window (click anywhere in the Data Editor).

2. From the menus choose:

> File
>   Save As...

This opens the Save Data As dialog box, as shown in Figure 3.7.

3. Enter a name for the data file in the File name text box and click Save to save the data file in SPSS format.

Figure 3.7   Save Data As dialog box

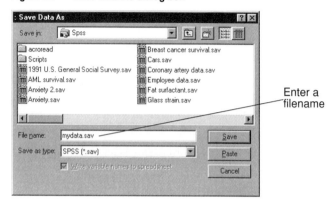

To save to a
floppy disk,
select a: or b:
from the drop-
down Save in
list.

Enter a
filename

By default, SPSS saves data files in SPSS format. For information on saving
(or reading) data files in other formats, see Chapter 9.

Additional Information

The following sections provide additional information that you might find
useful.

Missing Values

The data you want to use for analysis may not always contain complete information for every case. For example, some respondents may refuse to answer a certain survey question. SPSS provides two methods for handling missing values.

- **System-missing value**. If no value is entered for a numeric variable, SPSS assigns the system-missing value (represented by a period in the Data Editor).

- **User-missing values**. Data can be missing for a variety of reasons. If you
  know why particular data are missing, you can assign values that identify
  information missing for specific reasons and then instruct SPSS to flag these
  values as missing. To define user-missing values, use the Define Variable
  option on the Data menu, and select Missing Values in the Define Variable
  dialog box.

Variable Naming Rules

The basic rules for SPSS variable names are:

- The name must begin with a letter.
- Variable names cannot end with a period.
- The length of the variable name cannot exceed eight characters.
- Variable names cannot contain blanks or special characters (for example, !, ?, ', and *).
- Each variable name must be unique. Duplication is not allowed.
- Variable names are not case sensitive.

What's Next?

At this point, you can exit SPSS or continue with the next tutorial.

4 Working with Statistics and Output

This chapter introduces the use of the SPSS Statistics menu and Output Navigator and demonstrates the following:

- Opening a data file in the SPSS Data Editor
- Obtaining a crosstabulation of two variables
- Navigating, editing, and saving SPSS output

Opening an SPSS Data File

SPSS for Windows is able to open a number of different types of data files, including spreadsheet files created with Lotus 1-2-3, Excel, and Multiplan, dBASE files, and tab-delimited ASCII files. This tutorial uses the SPSS data file *Employee data.sav*.

❶ To open the *Employee data.sav* data file, from the menus choose:

File
  Open...

This opens the Open File dialog box, as shown in Figure 4.1.

Figure 4.1   Open File dialog box

If you can't find the data file, make sure that you are looking in the directory where SPSS is installed (usually c:\program files\spss) and that files with the .sav extension are listed.

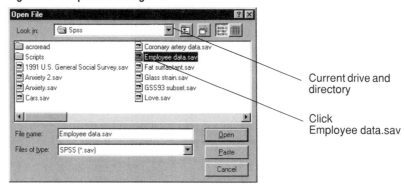

❷ Select *Employee data.sav* on the list of files.

❸ Click **Open** or press ↵Enter.

The data file is displayed in the Data Editor window, as shown in Figure 4.2. The appearance of the data file varies depending on whether or not value labels are displayed.

Figure 4.2   Data Editor windows (with and without value labels displayed)

You can display (or hide) value labels by clicking

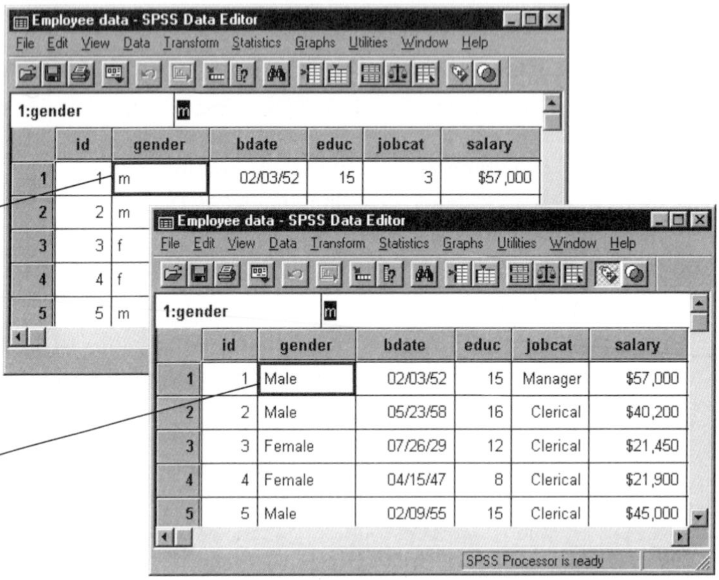

Value

Value label

The Employee Data File

Variables such as minority and jobcat use numeric codes to represent categorical information.

The file *Employee data.sav* contains historical data about a company's employees. The data were gathered as part of a study to determine whether the company had discriminated against women and minorities in its employment practices. The file contains the following variables:

- *id*—the employee's identification number (in order of hiring).

- *gender* —coded as follows: m=male, f=female.

Variables such as jobtime and salary represent actual numerical data.

- *minority*—the employee's minority status: 0=no, 1=yes.

- *bdate*—the date of birth for each employee.

- *educ*—the highest grade level completed by the employee: 12=high school diploma, 16=bachelor's degree, and so on.

- *jobcat*—the individual's employment category: 1=clerical, 2=custodial, 3=manager.

- *salary*—the employee's current salary, adjusted to 1992 dollars.
- *salbegin*—the employee's salary at time of hiring, in 1992 dollars.
- *jobtime*—the number of months the employee has been with the company.
- *prevexp* —employee's experience (in months) prior to joining the company.

Using Statistical Procedures

The Statistics menu contains a list of general statistical categories. The arrow (▶) following each menu selection indicates that there is an additional menu level. The individual statistical procedures are listed at this submenu level.

To examine the relationship between job category, gender, and minority among company employees, you can crosstabulate the variables *jobcat* and *gender* within categories of *minority*.

❶ To obtain a crosstabulation, from the menus choose:

Statistics
 Summarize ▶
  Crosstabs...

This opens the Crosstabs dialog box, as shown in Figure 4.3.

Figure 4.3   Crosstabs dialog box

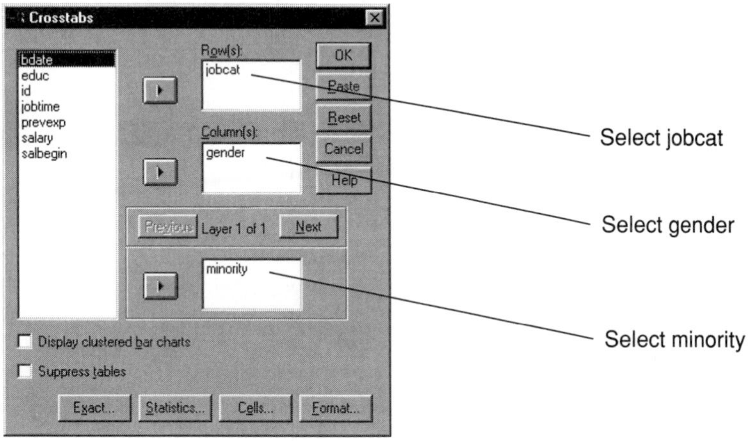

You can directly access variable information from any dialog box. Simply click on any variable with the right mouse button and then select Variable Information from the resulting menu.

Select jobcat

Select gender

Select minority

❷ Select *jobcat* on the variable list and click the ▶ pushbutton next to the Row(s) list box.

This moves *jobcat* to the Row(s) list.

❸ Select *gender* on the variable list and click the ▸ pushbutton next to the Column(s) list box.

This moves *gender* to the Column(s) list.

❹ Select *minority* on the variable list and click the ▸ pushbutton next to the Layer list box.

This moves *minority* to the Layer list. The dialog box should appear as shown in Figure 4.3 above.

❺ Click OK.

This closes the dialog box and runs the procedure.

The results—a crosstabulation for *jobcat* and *gender* within categories of *minority*—are displayed in the Output Navigator window, as shown in Figure 4.4.

Figure 4.4   Crosstabulation displayed in Output Navigator

You can use the maximize button and scroll bars to see more of the output.

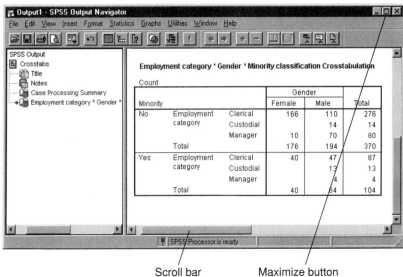

Scroll bar   Maximize button

Running Procedures with Additional Specifications

While running a procedure in SPSS, you can request additional specifications in subdialog boxes, which are accessed from the main dialog box.

In the output from the above crosstabulation, the distribution of gender and minority does not appear to be equal across different job categories. Most women (and *all* minority women) are clerical workers, while a large majority of managers are non-minority males. This suggests that there is a relationship between the variables *gender, minority,* and *jobcat.* But what is this relationship? And is it statistically significant?

To more closely examine the distribution of *gender* and *minority* across each value of *jobcat,* you can repeat the above crosstabulation, using an additional specification to display expected counts in each cell.

You can also reopen the dialog box by clicking on

❶ To obtain a crosstabulation with expected counts displayed in each cell, from the menus choose:

Statistics
  Summarize ▶
    Crosstabs...

This reopens the Crosstabs dialog box, as shown in Figure 4.3 on p. 27. (Notice that SPSS "remembers" your previous selections.)

❷ Move the variable *jobcat* to the Row(s) list if it is not already there.

❸ Move *gender* to the Column(s) list if it is not already there.

❹ Move *minority* to the Layer list if it is not already there.

❺ Click Cells... in the Crosstabs dialog box.

This opens the Crosstabs Cell Display dialog box, as shown in Figure 4.5.

Figure 4.5   Crosstabs Cell Display dialog box

Select Expected

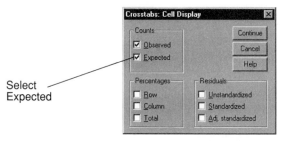

❻ Click Expected in the Counts group.

Expected counts will be displayed in each cell of the crosstabulation. The **expected count** is the number of observations that would occur in each cell if there were no relationship between the variables.

❼ Click Continue to close the Crosstabs Cell Display dialog box and return to the main Crosstabs dialog box.

❽ Click OK to run the procedure.

The results are displayed in the output window, as shown in Figure 4.6.

Figure 4.6   Crosstabulation with expected percentages

Minority				Female	Male	Total
No	Employment category	Clerical	Count	166	110	276
			Expected	131.3	144.7	276.0
		Custodial	Count	0	14	14
			Expected	6.7	7.3	14.0
		Manager	Count	10	70	80
			Expected	38.1	41.9	80.0
	Total		Count	176	194	370
			Expected	176.0	194.0	370.0
Yes	Employment category	Clerical	Count	40	47	87
			Expected	33.5	53.5	87.0
		Custodial	Count	0	13	13
			Expected	5.0	8.0	13.0
		Manager	Count	0	4	4
			Expected	1.5	2.5	4.0
	Total		Count	40	64	104
			Expected	40.0	64.0	104.0

The expected cell counts provide further indication that jobs may be unequally distributed across gender and minority categories. For example, there are almost twice as many non-minority males in salaried positions as you would expect if the variables were unrelated. The actual count is 70, while the expected count is only 41.9. Conversely, the expected number of minority females in clerical jobs is only 33.5, while the actual number is 40.

While the above crosstabulation suggests that a relationship does indeed exist between the variables, this analysis falls short of demonstrating that it is statistically significant.

Working with Output

Data analysis frequently requires numerous preliminary, exploratory steps, and many statistical procedures can generate a large volume of output. SPSS provides a number of facilities to help you navigate, edit, and save your results.

Navigating in the Output Navigator Window

When you run a procedure in SPSS, the results are displayed in a window called the Output Navigator. In this window, you can easily navigate to whichever part of the output you want to see.

To examine your output:

❶ Click anywhere in the Output Navigator to make it the active window. (You might also want to maximize the Output Navigator so that more of the output is visible.)

❷ Click on the first Crosstabs title in the outline pane to move to the output from the first Crosstabs procedure. Notice that a red arrow appears next to the Crosstabs table in the right pane and next to its title in the left pane (see Figure 4.7).

Figure 4.7   Output Navigator

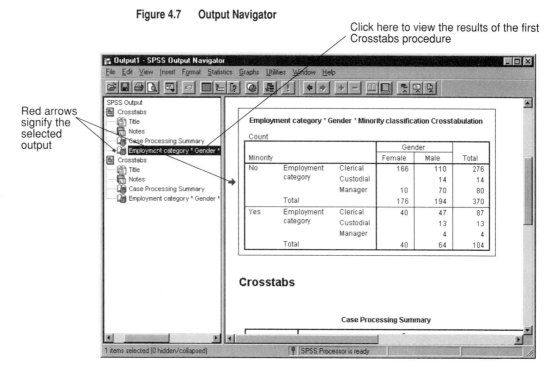

❸ Move to the output from the second Crosstabs procedure by clicking on its title in the outline pane. Alternatively, you can use the scroll bar to move to it.

Modifying Pivot Tables

The Crosstabs procedure (and most other statistical procedures in the Base system) produces output in the form of pivot tables. With pivot tables you can:

- Transpose rows and columns
- Move rows and columns
- Create multidimensional layers

To pivot a table or make other modifications:

❶ Double-click the the first Crosstabs table to activate it.

❷ From the menus choose:

Pivot
  Pivoting Trays

Figure 4.8   Activated pivot table with pivoting trays

Pivoting trays

Pivot icon for
minority

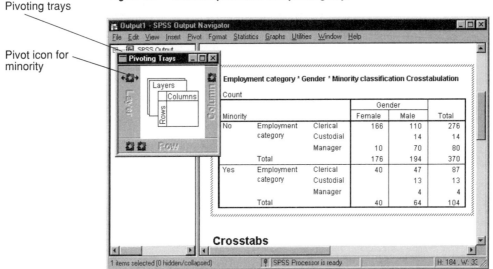

❸ Click on any pivot icon in the pivoting trays to identify the table dimension represented by the icon. The selected dimension appears shaded in the pivot table.

❹ Click and drag the pivot icon for *minority* from the Row dimension to the Layer dimension. This means that instead of having all the information in one table, there are two tables—one on top of the other.

The table now contains multiple layers, with each category of *minority* contained in a separate layer; so each layer displays a crosstabulation of *gender* and *jobcat* for a different category of *minority*.

⑤ Click the arrows on the pivot icon for *minority* to change the displayed layer.

Figure 4.9   Pivot table with layers

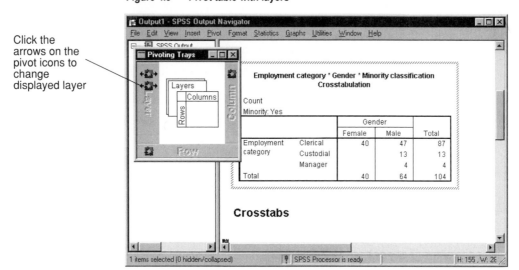

Click the arrows on the pivot icons to change displayed layer

You can also change the display order of rows or columns in a pivot table.

⑥ Click and drag the column label *Male* on top of the column label *Female*.

⑦ Choose Swap from the pop-up menu.

The positions of the two columns are now switched.

Customizing SPSS Output with Scripts

SPSS provides a scripting facility which enables you to automate many tasks, including modifying pivot tables. You can create your own scripts or use and modify the scripts that are included with SPSS.

Note: Scripting is not available in the Student Version.

❶ Click the crosstabulation pivot table (either one) to select it. (Don't double-click the table; you want only to select it, not to activate it.)

❷ From the menus choose:

Utilities
　Run Script...

③ From the Scripts directory, select *Make totals bold.sbs.*

Figure 4.10   Using scripts to customize output

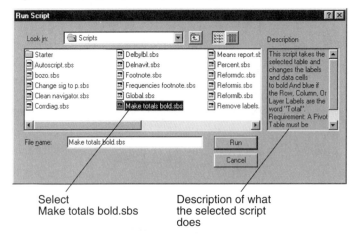

Select
Make totals bold.sbs

Description of what
the selected script
does

④ Click Run to run the script.

The totals row and column are now displayed in bold (and blue).

Figure 4.11   Bold totals using a script

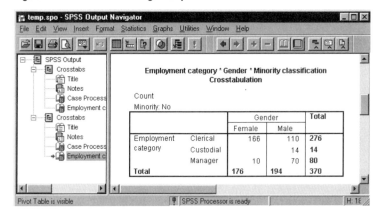

Autoscripts

An autoscript file is a collection of script subroutines that run automatically each time you run procedures that create certain types of output objects. SPSS comes with an autoscript file that contains the following routines:

Correlations_Table_Correlations_Create. In the correlation matrix from Bivariate Correlations, highlights significant correlation coefficients ($p<0.01$) and removes the upper diagonal of the correlation matrix.

Crosstabs_Table_Crosstabulation_Create. In crosstabulations from the Crosstabs procedure that contain row, column, or total percentages, changes labels to Row %, Column %, and Total %.

Descriptives_Table_DescriptiveStatistics_Create. In the Descriptives procedure, swaps the rows and columns of the table so that the statistics are in the rows and variables are in the columns.

Tables_Table_Table_Create. In tables produced by the Tables option, centers pivot tables in the Output Navigator (affects only printed output, not the display in the Output Navigator).

To activate the autoscript file and autoscript subroutines:

1 From the menus choose:
Edit
  Options...

2 Click the Scripts tab.

3 Select Enable Autoscripting.

4 Select the autoscript subroutines that you want to enable.

5 You can also specify a different autoscript file or global procedure file.

Saving Output

To save an Output Navigator document:

1 From the Output Navigator menus choose:
File
  Save

2 Type a name for the document and click Save.

To save output in external formats (for example, HTML or text), use Export on the File menu.

Pasting Output into Another Application

You can paste your output into another Windows application, such as a word processing program.

- To copy and paste a single output table or chart, select the item (click it once to select it, and choose Copy from the Edit menu. In the target application, choose Paste from the Edit menu. The item is pasted as a metafile or a bit-map, depending on the other application. Use Paste Special in the other application to control the pasted format.

- To copy and paste multiple output items, select the items (Shift-click or Ctrl-click to select multiple items), and choose Copy objects from the Edit menu. In the target application, choose Paste from the Edit menu.

- To paste pivot tables as text in another application, choose Paste Special from the Edit menu in the target application, and then select Unformatted text.

Finding Information about Variables

SPSS provides several ways to easily keep track of variable definition information.

- In most SPSS dialog boxes, click on any listed variable name with the *right* mouse button, then select Variable Information from the menu to pop up a window displaying any variable and value labels defined for that variable.

- For complete information about all of the variables in the current data file, choose Variables from the Utilities menu. This opens the Variables window, as shown in Figure 4.12. For further instructions, click Help in the Variables window.

Figure 4.12   Variables window

You can also open the Variables window by clicking .

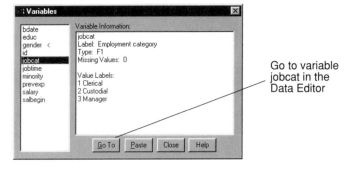

Go to variable jobcat in the Data Editor

What's Next?

At this point, you can exit from SPSS or continue with the next tutorial. If you exit from SPSS and you have changed the data file in any way, you will be asked whether you want to save the changes. *Do not* save changes to the *Employee data.sav* data file.

5 Tutorial: Creating Bar Charts

This tutorial introduces the basics of creating charts using the SPSS Graphs menu and demonstrates the following:

- Creating a simple bar chart summarizing groups of cases
- Creating a simple bar chart summarizing separate variables
- Creating a clustered bar chart

This tutorial uses the file *Employee data.sav*, described in previous chapters. If you need help in opening the file, see Chapter 4.

Creating a Chart Summarizing Groups of Cases

Figure 5.1 shows a simple bar chart that plots the mean salary for employees within each job category.

Figure 5.1   Simple bar chart

A single categorical variable (jobcat) is summarized. Each bar represents the mean salary for a group of cases.

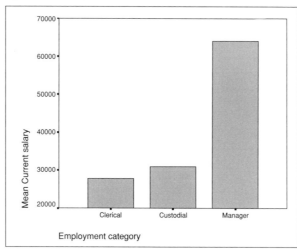

❶ To create the above bar chart, from the menus choose:

Graphs
  Bar...

This opens the Bar Charts dialog box, as shown in Figure 5.2.

Figure 5.2   Bar Charts dialog box

Already
selected

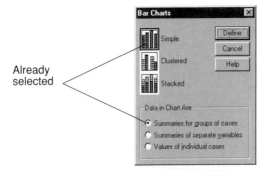

The option for a simple bar chart should already be selected, as well as the option Summaries for groups of cases, which is used to summarize a variable within categories.

❷ Click Define.

This opens the Define Simple Bar Summaries for Groups of Cases dialog box, as shown in Figure 5.3.

Figure 5.3   Define Simple Bar Summaries for Groups of Cases dialog box

Each bar will represent the mean salary within a single job category.

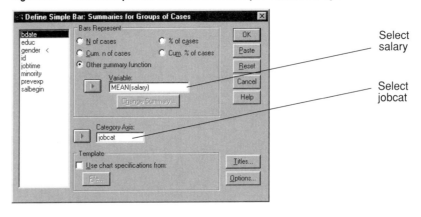

Select salary

Select jobcat

③ In the Bars Represent group, select Other summary function. Select *salary* for the summary function variable.

MEAN(salary) appears in the Variable box.

④ Select *jobcat* for Category Axis.

There will be a separate bar for each job category.

⑤ Click OK.

The chart is displayed in the Output Navigator, as shown in Figure 5.4.

Figure 5.4   Simple bar chart in the Output Navigator

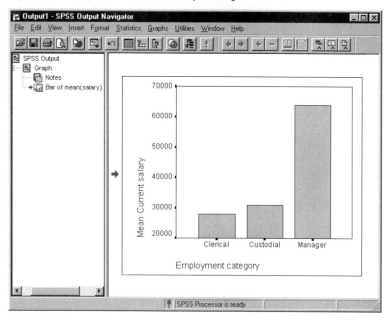

Creating a Chart Summarizing Separate Variables

Suppose you now want to compare beginning and current salaries. You can create a bar chart that shows mean current and beginning salaries for all employees.

① From the menus choose:

Graphs
  Bar...

This opens the Bar Charts dialog box, as shown in Figure 5.5.

Figure 5.5   Bar Charts dialog box

Select
Summaries of
separate
variables

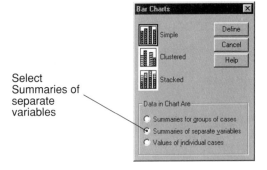

② In the Data in Chart Are group, select Summaries of separate variables.

③ Click Define.

This opens the Define Simple Bar Summaries of Separate Variables dialog box, as shown in Figure 5.6.

Figure 5.6   Define Simple Bar Summaries of Separate Variables dialog box

*Each bar will
represent the
mean of a
separate variable
across all cases.*

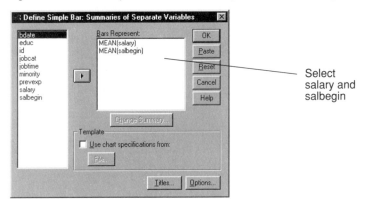

Select
salary and
salbegin

④ Select *salary* on the variable list and click ▶.

MEAN(salary) appears on the Bars Represent list.

⑤ Select *salbegin* and click ▶ again.

MEAN(salbegin) appears on the Bars Represent list.

⑥ Click OK.

SPSS displays the chart in the Output Navigator (see Figure 5.7).

Figure 5.7   Bar chart of salary and salbegin in the Output Navigator

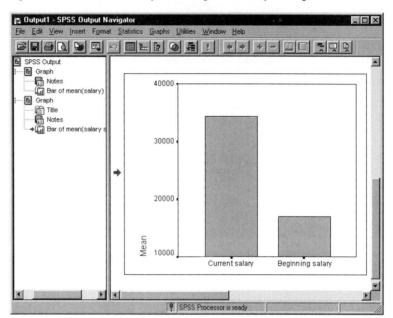

*Each bar
represents the
mean of a
separate variable.*

Creating a Clustered Bar Chart

In a clustered bar chart, there is a cluster of bars (rather than a single bar) for each point on the category axis. Figure 5.8 shows a clustered bar chart that plots the number of males and females within each job category.

Figure 5.8   Clustered bar chart

There is a cluster of bars for each point on the category axis.

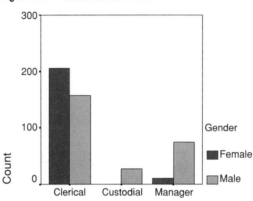

To create the clustered bar chart shown above:

❶ From the menus choose:

Graphs
  Bar...

This opens the Bar Charts dialog box, as shown in Figure 5.9.

Figure 5.9   Bar Charts dialog box

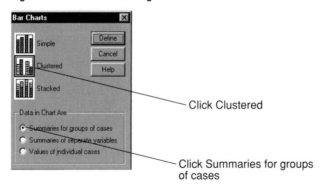

2 To create a clustered bar chart, click Clustered.

3 In the Data in Chart Are group, select Summaries for groups of cases.

In this example, cases are first grouped according to job category and then further grouped within each job category according to gender.

4 Click Define.

This opens the Define Clustered Bar Summaries for Groups of Cases dialog box, as shown in Figure 5.10.

Figure 5.10   Define Clustered Bar Summaries for Groups of Cases dialog box

Categories of gender will be summarized within categories of jobcat.

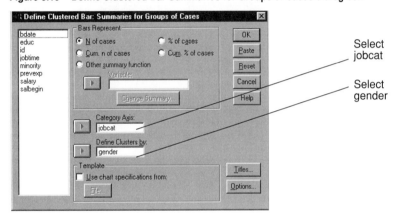

In the Bars Represent group, the default N of cases will chart the number of cases in each of the categories.

5 Select *jobcat* for Category Axis.

There will be a separate cluster of bars for each job category.

6 Select *gender* for Define Clusters by.

Within each cluster, there will be a separate bar for males and females.

7 Click OK.

Figure 5.11 shows the resulting chart.

Figure 5.11   Clustered bar chart in the Output Navigator

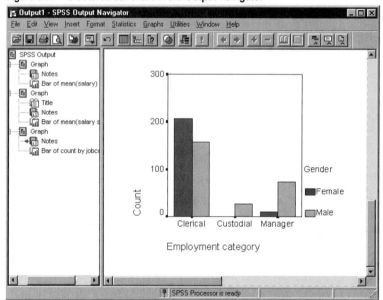

Pasting Charts into Another Application

To copy and paste a chart into another application, such as a word processing program:

1. Select the chart in the Output Navigator (click on the chart once to select it).

2. From the menus choose:

   Edit
     Copy

   This copies the chart to the Windows clipboard in metafile and bitmap format.

3. Position the cursor in the target application where you want to place the chart.

4. From the target application's menus choose:

   Edit
     Paste Special...

5. From the Paste Special dialog box, select Picture or Bitmap.

What's Next?

At this point, you can choose to continue experimenting with the Graphs menu, continue with the next tutorial (where you will learn how to edit charts), or exit SPSS. If you exit SPSS, *do not* save any changes to the *Employee data.sav* file.

6

Tutorial: Creating and Modifying a Scatterplot

This tutorial introduces the basics of editing charts in a chart window and demonstrates the following:

- Creating a scatterplot
- Moving the scatterplot from the Output Navigator into a chart window
- Using point selection mode to identify points in the scatterplot
- Changing the scale of the *x*-axis
- Adding a regression line and title to the scatterplot

Creating a Scatterplot

A scatterplot shows the relationship between two continuous variables, such as *salary* and *salbegin*.

1 Open the file *Employee data.sav*, which is described in previous chapters. If you need help opening the file, see Chapter 4.

2 To create a scatterplot that shows the relationship between beginning and current salary, from the menus choose:

Graphs
  Scatter...

This opens the Scatterplot dialog box, as shown in Figure 6.1. (The Simple chart type is selected by default).

Figure 6.1   Scatterplot dialog box

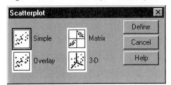

❸ Click Define.

This opens the Simple Scatterplot dialog box, as shown in Figure 6.2.

Figure 6.2   Simple Scatterplot dialog box

Select salary

Select salbegin

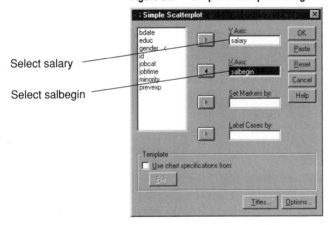

❹ Select *salary* for the Y Axis and select *salbegin* for the X Axis.

❺ Click OK.

The chart is displayed in the Output Navigator, as shown in Figure 6.3.

Figure 6.3   Scatterplot in the Output Navigator

Double-click on the chart to edit the scatterplot

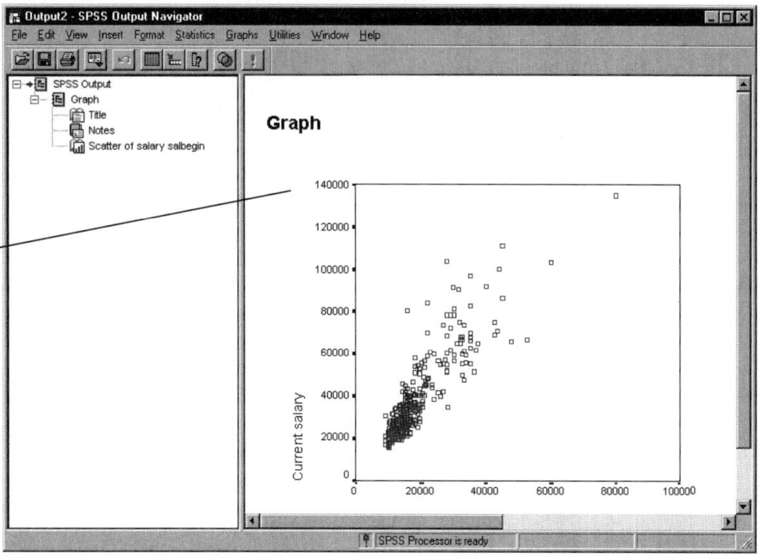

Editing the Chart

You can have more than one Chart Editor window open at one time. Each chart is displayed in a separate window.

To modify the chart:

❶ Double-click the chart in the Output Navigator. This opens a chart editor window containing the scatterplot, as shown in Figure 6.4, with the Chart Editor menu bar and toolbar displayed.

Figure 6.4   Scatterplot in a chart window

Chart Editor
menu bar
and toolbar

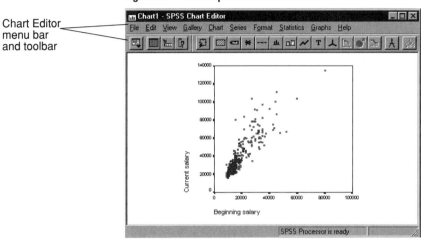

Using Point Selection Mode to Identify Points

Examining your scatterplot, you notice one person whose salary has increased
from roughly $30,000 to more that $100,000 (as indicated in Figure 6.5). To
find out more about this individual, you can use point selection mode.

Figure 6.5   Scatterplot in a chart window

*With a boxplot
or scatterplot in
theactive chart
window, click*

 .

*The cursor
changes to*

 ,

*which indicates
tha point
selection is on.*

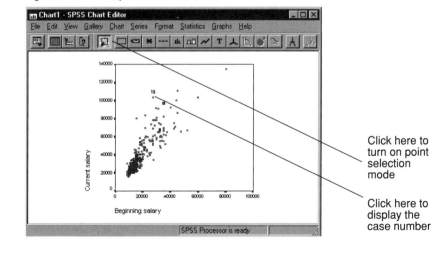

Click here to
turn on point
selection
mode

Click here to
display the
case number

❷ Click 🔲 on the toolbar.

This turns on point selection mode.

❸ Click on the point indicated in Figure 6.5.

The value 18 is displayed, indicating that the case in question is case number 18.

❹ Click 🔳 on the toolbar.

This activates the Data Editor, with case number 18 selected, as shown in Figure 6.6.

Figure 6.6   Data Editor with case selected

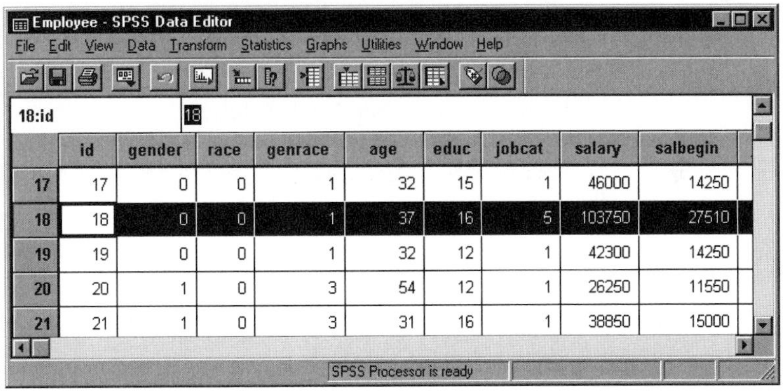

	id	gender	race	genrace	age	educ	jobcat	salary	salbegin
17	17	0	0	1	32	15	1	46000	14250
18	18	0	0	1	37	16	5	103750	27510
19	19	0	0	1	32	12	1	42300	14250
20	20	1	0	3	54	12	1	26250	11550
21	21	1	0	3	31	16	1	38850	15000

❺ After you are finished examining the data, click 🔲 to return to the scatterplot.

❻ Click on point number 18 again to deselect it.

The displayed value 18 disappears.

❼ Click 🔲 again.

This turns off point selection mode.

Adding a Regression Line

The scatterplot appears to be linear.

❽ To draw a line that fits the distribution of points, from the menus choose:

Chart
  Options...

This opens the Scatterplot Options dialog box, as shown in Figure 6.7.

Figure 6.7   Scatterplot Options dialog box

Click Total

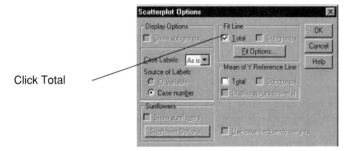

9 In the Fit Line group, click Total.

All of the points will be used when the position of the line is calculated.

10 Click OK.

This places a regression line on the scatterplot. (Figure 6.10 on p. 55 shows the finished scatterplot.)

Changing the Scale Axis

Suppose you want to see cases with beginning salaries below $40,000 in more detail. You can change the scale of the *x*-axis so that only these cases are displayed.

11 Double-click on one of the numbers in the horizontal axis (or choose Axis from the Chart menu, select X scale, and click OK).

This opens the X Scale Axis dialog box, as shown in Figure 6.8.

Figure 6.8   X Scale Axis dialog box

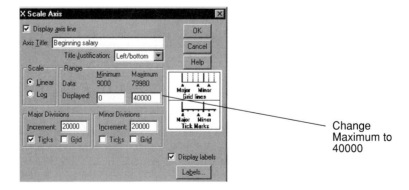

Change Maximum to 40000

⑫ In the Range box, change the maximum displayed from 100000 to 40000, then click OK.

Figure 6.10 below shows the finished scatterplot.

Adding a Title

You can customize your chart by adding a title.

⑬ To add a title to the chart, from the menus choose:

Chart
  Title...

This opens the Titles dialog box, as shown in Figure 6.9.

Figure 6.9   Titles dialog box

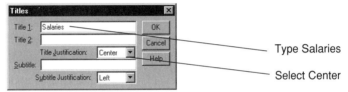

⑭ Type **Salaries** in the Title 1 text box.

⑮ To center the title, select Center from the Title Justification drop-down list.

⑯ Click OK.

The title is displayed, as shown in Figure 6.10.

Figure 6.10   Scatterplot with regression line, title, and modified x-axis

Although cases with beginning salaries greater than $40,000 are not displayed, they are still used to calculate the regression line.

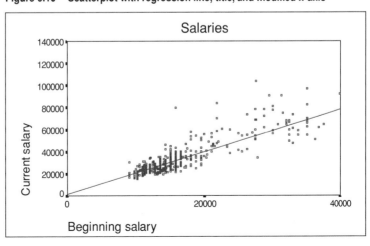

What's Next?

At this point, you can choose to continue experimenting with the Graphs menu, continue with the next tutorial, or exit SPSS. If you exit SPSS, *do not* save any changes to the *Employee data.sav* data file.

7 Tutorial: Modifying Data Values

SPSS provides numerous facilities for modifying data values and creating new variables based on transformations of existing variables. This tutorial introduces the use of the SPSS Transform menu and demonstrates the use of the Recode option to recode a continuous variable into distinct categories.

Recoding Data Values

One of the most useful data transformations is accomplished with the Recode facility, which is used to combine categories of a variable.

For example, you can't use actual salaries in a crosstabulation to show the relationship between salary and gender because very few people are likely to have the same salary. The number of distinct "categories" for salary would likely be almost as large as the number of cases in your data file. You could, however, create a new variable that combines salary ranges into a small number of categories, such as less than $25,000, $25,000 to $49,999, and $50,000 or more.

❶ Open the file *Employee data.sav*, which is described in previous chapters. If you need help opening the file, see Chapter 4.

❷ From the menus choose:

Transform
  Recode ▶
    Into Different Variables...

This opens the Recode into Different Variables dialog box.

❸ Select *salary* on the variable list and click ▶ to move it to the Numeric Variable -> Output Variable list, as shown in Figure 7.1.

Figure 7.1   Recode into Different Variables dialog box

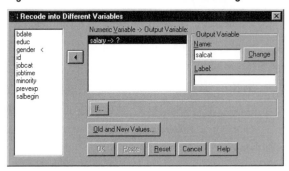

To recode a string
variable into
consecutive
integer values,
you can use the
Automatic
Recode option on
the Transform
menu.

④ In the Output Variable group, type **salcat** in the Name text box.

⑤ Click Change.

The original variable name and the new variable name are displayed together on the Numeric Variable -> Output Variable list.

⑥ Click Old and New Values....

This opens the Old and New Values dialog box, as shown in Figure 7.2.

Figure 7.2   Old and New Values dialog box

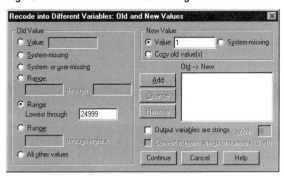

⑦ In the Old Value group, select Range: Lowest through.

⑧ Type **24999** in the Lowest through text box.

⑨ In the New Value group, select Value.

⑩ Type **1** in the Value text box.

⑪ Click Add.

Lowest thru 24999 --> 1 is displayed on the Old --> New list (see Figure 7.3). This means that all salaries below $25,000 will be combined into a single category coded 1 for the new variable *salcat*.

12 In the Old Value group, select Range.

13 Type **25000** in the first Range text box.

14 Type **49999** in the second Range text box.

15 In the New Value group, select Value, type **2** in the text box, and then click Add.

16 In the Old Value group, select Range: through highest and type **50000** in the text box.

17 In the New Value group, select Value, type **3** in the text box, and then click Add.

The Old and New Values dialog box should now look like Figure 7.3.

Figure 7.3   Completed Old and New Values dialog box

Any unspecified old values will be set to system-missing for the new variable. If you don't want to recode all values, select All other values and select Copy old value(s) to retain values not covered by the recoding scheme.

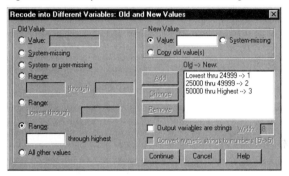

18 Click Continue in the Old and New Values dialog box, and then click OK in the main Recode into Different Variables dialog box.

If SPSS does not calculate values for the new variable after you click OK, choose Run Pending Transformations from the Transform menu.

The new variable *salcat* is added to the data file and is the last column displayed in the Data Editor window. You can add descriptive value labels for the numeric category codes by using the Define Variable option on the Data menu (see Chapter 3 for more information on defining variables).

Note: If SPSS does not calculate values for the new variable after you click OK, choose Run Pending Transformations from the Transform menu. (If you want SPSS to always run your transformations immediately, choose Preferences from the Edit menu. In the Preferences dialog box, be sure that the option Calculate values immediately is selected in the Transformation and Merge Options group.)

What's Next?

At this point, you can exit SPSS or continue with the next tutorial. If you exit SPSS and you have changed the data file in any way, you will be asked whether you want to save the changes. *Do not* save changes to the data file *Employee data.sav*.

Note: If you want to save the data file with the new variable created in this tutorial, you should use the Save As option on the File menu and give the file a new name.

8 Tutorial: Working with Syntax

This tutorial introduces the use of command syntax, an alternate way to run procedures. Using syntax also allows you to save the exact specifications used during an SPSS session. This tutorial demonstrates the following:

- Pasting syntax from a dialog box
- Typing syntax into a syntax window
- Editing syntax

Note: Syntax is not available in the Student Version.

Pasting Syntax

The easiest way to construct a useful command is to paste the syntax from a dialog box. In this example, command syntax will be used to run the Frequencies procedure. The results are similar to those shown in Chapter 1.

1 Open the file *Employee data.sav*, which is described in previous chapters. If you need help opening the file, see Chapter 4.

2 From the menus choose:

Statistics
  Summarize
    Frequencies...

This opens the Frequencies dialog box.

3 Select *jobcat* and move it to the Variable(s) list.

4 Click Charts....

5 In the Charts dialog box, select Bar charts, and in the Chart Values group, select Percentages. Then click Continue.

The Frequencies dialog box is displayed, as shown in Figure 8.1.

Figure 8.1   Frequencies dialog box

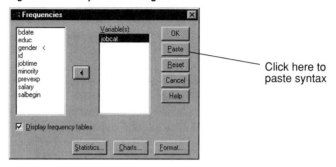

Click here to
paste syntax

6 Click Paste (instead of OK).

This opens a syntax window and pastes the FREQUENCIES command into it,
as shown in Figure 8.2.

Figure 8.2   Syntax window

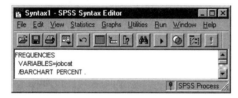

*To run several
commands,
highlight the
commands and
click*

.

7 To run the command, make sure the cursor is within the command, and click
the Run Syntax tool   .

The results are the same as if you had clicked OK in the Frequencies dialog box.

Editing Syntax

In the syntax window, you can edit the syntax. For example, you could change the subcommand /BARCHART to display frequencies instead of percentages, as shown in Figure 8.3. (A subcommand is indicated by a slash.)

Figure 8.3   Modified syntax

To find out what subcommands and keywords are available for the current command, click the Syntax Help tool 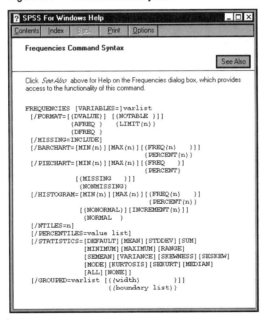. Complete syntax for the FREQUENCIES command is shown in Figure 8.4.

Figure 8.4   FREQUENCIES syntax

If the cursor is not in a command, clicking the Syntax Help tool displays an alphabetical list of commands. You can click the one you want.

Typing Syntax

You can type syntax into a syntax window that is already open, or you can open a new syntax window by choosing:

File
  New
    Syntax

Saving Syntax

To save a syntax file, from the menus choose:

File
  Save

or

File
  Save As...

This opens a standard Windows dialog box for saving files.

Opening and Running a Syntax File

To open a saved syntax file, from the menus choose:

File
  Open

Select a syntax file and click Open (if no syntax files are displayed, make sure Syntax (*.sps) is selected in the Files of Type drop-down menu). Then run the commands by using the Run Syntax tool, as described above. If the commands apply to a specific data file, the data file must be opened before running the commands, or you must include a command that opens the data file. You can paste this type of command from the dialog boxes that open data files.

Additional Information

In the Help system, most procedures have a topic that discusses additional features available with command language. For more information about how to use syntax, you can search the Help system for Syntax. You can also consult the *SPSS Base System Syntax Reference Guide* that comes with SPSS for Windows.

What's Next?

At this point, you can exit SPSS. When you exit SPSS and you have changed the data file in any way, you will be asked whether you want to save the changes. *Do not* save changes to the data file *Employee data.sav*.

The next chapter describes data files in different formats.

9 Data Files

SPSS is designed to handle a wide variety of formats, including:

- Spreadsheet files created with Lotus 1-2-3, Excel, and Multiplan
- Database files created with dBASE
- Tab-delimited and other types of ASCII text files
- SPSS data files created on other operating systems
- SYSTAT data files

Creating a New Data File

If your data are not already in computer files, you can use the Data Editor to enter the data and create an SPSS data file. The Data Editor is a simple, efficient spreadsheet-like facility that opens automatically when you start an SPSS session. For information about the Data Editor, see Chapter 3.

Opening a Data File

To open a data file from the menus in the Data Editor window choose:

File
  Open...

This opens the Open File dialog box, as shown in Figure 9.1.

Figure 9.1   Open File dialog box

If the extension of your data file is different from the default extension for the file type, select the file type from the File of type drop-down list or type an asterisk (*) followed by the file extension in the File name field.

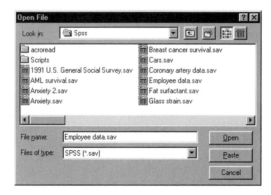

Specifying File Type

By default, SPSS displays a list of data files saved in SPSS format (*.sav). To display a list of files in other formats, select the file format from the drop-down list of file types.

Reading Variable Names

For Lotus, Excel, SYLK, and tab-delimited files, you can read variable names from the file. The values in the first row of the file (or cell range) are used as variable names. If variable names exceed eight characters, they are truncated. If they are not unique, SPSS modifies them.

Reading a Range of Cells

For Lotus, Excel, and SYLK files, you can specify a range of cells to read.

- For Lotus files, specify the beginning column letter and row number, two periods, and the ending column letter and row number (for example, A1..K14).

- For Excel files, specify the beginning column letter and row number, a colon, and the ending column letter and row number (for example, A1:K14).

- For SYLK files and Excel files saved in R1C1 display format, specify the beginning and ending cells of the range separated by a colon (for example, R1C1:R14C11).

If you have defined a name for a range of cells in the spreadsheet file, you can enter the name in the Range text box.

How SPSS Reads Spreadsheet Data

An SPSS data file is rectangular. The boundaries (or dimensions) of the data file are determined by the number of cases (rows) and variables (columns). There are no "empty" cells within the boundaries of the data file. All cells have a value, even if that value is "blank." The following general rules apply to reading spreadsheet data:

If your spreadsheet is organized with cases in columns and variables in rows, use the Transpose option on the Data menu to put your data in the correct order after you read the data into SPSS.

- Rows are considered cases, and columns are considered variables.

- The number of variables is determined by the last column with any non-blank cells or the total number of nonblank cells in the row containing variable names. If you read variable names, any columns with a blank cell for the variable name are not included in the data file.

- The number of cases is determined by the last row with any nonblank cells within the column boundaries defined by the number of variables (unless you read a range of cells).

- The data type and width for each variable are determined by the column width and data type of the first data cell in the column. Values of other types are converted to the system-missing value. If the first data cell in the column is blank, the global default data type for the spreadsheet (usually numeric) is used.

- For numeric variables, blank cells are converted to the system-missing value, indicated by a period.

- For string variables, a blank is a valid string value, and blank cells are treated as valid string values.

- If you do not read variable names from the spreadsheet, SPSS uses the column letters (A, B, C, etc.) for variable names for Excel and Lotus files. For SYLK files and Excel files saved in R1C1 display format, SPSS uses the column number preceded by the letter C for variable names (*C1*, *C2*, *C3*, etc.).

Figure 9.2 shows how SPSS reads a spreadsheet file that contains variable names, and Figure 9.3 shows how SPSS reads an Excel spreadsheet file that has no variable names.

Figure 9.2   Reading spreadsheet data with variable names

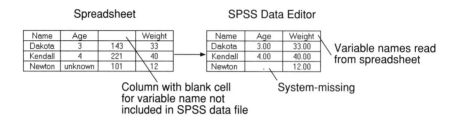

Figure 9.3   Reading Excel spreadsheet file without variable names

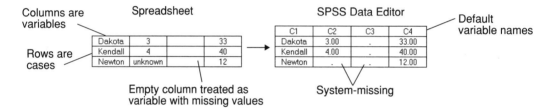

How SPSS Reads dBASE Files

Database files are logically very similar to SPSS data files. The following general rules apply to dBASE files:

- Field names are automatically translated to SPSS variable names.

- Field names should comply with SPSS variable-naming conventions (see "Defining Fixed Variables" on p. 72). Field names longer than eight characters are truncated. If the first eight characters of the field name do not produce a unique name, the field is dropped.

- Colons used in dBASE field names are translated to underscores.

- Records marked for deletion but not actually purged are included. SPSS creates a new string variable, *D_R*, which contains an asterisk for cases marked for deletion.

How SPSS Reads Tab-Delimited Files

The following general rules apply to reading tab-delimited files:

- Values can be either numeric or string. Any value that contains non-numeric characters is considered a string value. (Formats such as Dollar and Date are not recognized and are read as string values.)

- The data type and width for each variable are determined by the type and width of the first data value in the column. Values of other types are converted to the system-missing value.

- For numeric variables, the assigned width is eight digits or the number of digits in the first data value, whichever is greater. Values that exceed the defined width are rounded for display. The entire value is stored internally.

- For string variables, values that exceed the defined width are truncated.

- If you do not read variable names from the file, SPSS assigns the default names *var1*, *var2*, *var3*, etc.

Reading Text Files

If your raw data are in simple text files (standard ASCII format), you can read the data in SPSS and assign variable names and data formats. To read a text file, from the menus choose:

File
  Read ASCII Data
    Freefield

or

File
  Read ASCII Data
    Fixed Columns

Freefield. The variables are recorded in the same order for each case, but not necessarily in the same locations. Spaces are interpreted as delimiters between values. More than one case can be recorded on a single line. After reading the value for the last defined variable for a case, SPSS reads the next value encountered as the first variable for the next case.

Fixed Columns. Each variable is recorded in the same column location on the same record (line) for each case in the data file. This is the default.

Defining Fixed Variables

The Define Fixed Variables dialog box is shown in Figure 9.4.

Figure 9.4   Define Fixed Variables dialog box

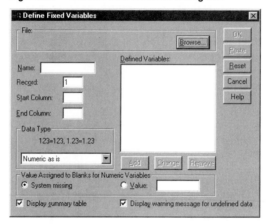

For each variable, you must specify the following:

Name. Variable names must begin with a letter and cannot exceed eight characters. Each variable name must be unique. Variable names are not case sensitive.

Record. A case can have data on more than one line. The **record number** indicates the line within the case where the variable is located.

Start Column/End Column. These two column specifications indicate the location of the variable within the record. The value for a variable can appear anywhere within the range of columns. With the exception of string variables, leading blank spaces in the column range are ignored.

Data Type. Select a data type from the drop-down list. When you select a data type, an example is displayed above the drop-down list.

Entering Variable Definitions

To enter a variable definition:

1. Specify the variable name, record, column locations, and data type.

2. Click Add. The record number, start and end columns, variable name, and data type appear on the Defined Variables list, as shown in Figure 9.5.

Figure 9.5   Defined Variables

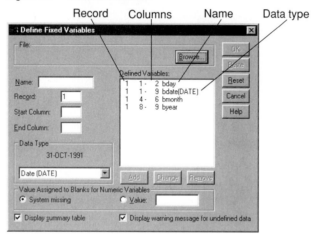

The following general rules apply:

- You can enter variables in any order. They are automatically sorted by record and start column.

- You can specify multiple variables in the same or overlapping column locations. For example, in Figure 9.5, *bday* is in columns 1–2, *bmonth* in columns 4–6, *byear* in columns 8–9, and *bdate* in columns 1–9.

- You can read selective data fields and/or records. You do not have to define or read all the data in the file. SPSS reads only the columns and records you specify and skips over any data you do not define.

Defining Freefield Variables

The Define Freefield Variables dialog box is shown in Figure 9.6.

Figure 9.6   Define Freefield Variables dialog box

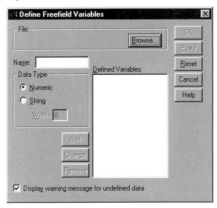

For each variable, you must specify the following:

Name. Variable names must begin with a letter and cannot exceed eight characters. Additional variable naming rules are given in "Defining Fixed Variables" on p. 72.

Data Type. For freefield format, data can be either numeric or string (alphanumeric).

Entering Variable Definitions

To enter a variable definition, specify the variable name and data type and click Add. The variable appears on the Defined Variables list. If it is a string variable, the letter A and the defined width appear in parentheses next to the variable name.

While defining data in freefield format is relatively simple and easy, it is also easy to make mistakes. Keep the following rules in mind:

- You must enter variables in the order in which they appear in the data file. Each new variable definition is added to the bottom of the list, and SPSS reads the variables in that order.

- You must provide definitions for all variables in the file. If you omit any, the data file will be read incorrectly. SPSS determines the end of one case and the beginning of the next based on the number of defined variables.

- The data file cannot contain any missing data. Blank fields are read as delimiters between variables, and SPSS does not distinguish between single and multiple blanks. If a single observation is missing, the entire remainder of the data file will be read incorrectly.

- If your Windows International settings (accessed from the Control Panel) use a period as the decimal indicator, SPSS interprets commas as delimiters that separate data values in freefield format. For example, a value of 1,234 is read as two separate values: 1 and 234.

Saving a Data File

You can save data files in any of the following formats:

- SPSS
- SPSS/PC+
- SPSS portable format (for use on other operating systems)
- Lotus 1-2-3
- Excel
- SYLK (symbolic link)
- dBASE
- Tab-delimited ASCII text
- Fixed-format ASCII text

To save a new SPSS data file or to save the data in a different file format:

1. Make the Data Editor the active window (by clicking anywhere in the Data Editor).

2. From the menus choose:

   File
     Save As...

This opens the Save Data As dialog box, as shown in Figure 9.7.

Figure 9.7   Save Data As dialog box

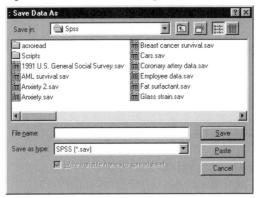

Specifying File Type

Before you can save a data file, you need to tell SPSS what type of file it is. SPSS needs to know the file type regardless of the file extension. To change the file type, you must change the selection on the drop-down list. You cannot specify a different file type simply by changing the extension of the wildcard search in the File name text box.

Closing a Data File

Since only one data file can be open at a time, SPSS automatically closes the working data file before it opens another one. If there have been any changes to the data file since it was last saved, SPSS asks if you want to save the changes before it closes the file and opens the next one.

10 Calculating New Data Values

In an ideal situation, your raw data are perfectly suitable for the type of analysis you want to perform. Unfortunately, this is rarely the case. Preliminary analysis may reveal inconvenient coding schemes or coding errors, or data transformations may be required in order to coax out the true relationship between variables.

With SPSS, you can perform data transformations ranging from simple tasks, such as collapsing categories for analysis, to creating new variables based on complex equations and conditional statements.

Recoding Values

You can modify data values by recoding them. This is particularly useful for combining categories. You can recode the values within existing variables, or you can create new variables based on the recoded values of existing variables. For more information about recoding, see Chapter 7.

Computing Values

To compute values for a variable based on numeric transformations of other variables, from the menus choose:

Transform
  Compute...

This opens the Compute Variable dialog box, as shown in Figure 10.1.

Figure 10.1   Compute Variable dialog box

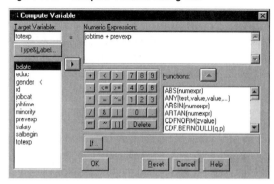

To compute a variable:

1. Enter a target variable name. If you enter an existing variable name, the computed values replace the original values.

2. Enter the numeric expression for the computed value. If the computed value is based on the values of existing variables, you can select the variable names from the variable list.

For example, in Figure 10.1, the new variable *totexp* will be computed as the sum of variables *jobtime* and *prevexp*.

Calculator Pad

The calculator pad contains numbers, arithmetic operators, relational operators, and logical operators (see Table 10.1). You can use it like a calculator (using the mouse to point and click on keys) or simply as a reference for the correct symbols to use for various operators.

Table 10.1 Calculator pad operators

Arithmetic Operators		Relational Operators		Logical Operators	
+	Addition	<	Less than	&	And. Both relations must be true.
–	Subtraction	>	Greater than	|	Or. Either relation can be true.
*	Multiplication	<=	Less than or equal to	~	Not. Reverses the true/false outcome of the expression.
/	Division	>=	Greater than or equal to		
**	Exponentiation	=	Equal to		
( )	Order of operations	~=	Not equal to		

Arithmetic Operators

Since fairly complex expressions are possible, it is important to keep in mind the order in which operations are performed. Functions are evaluated first, followed by exponentiation, then multiplication and division, and finally addition and subtraction. You can control the order of operations by enclosing in parentheses the operation you want to be executed first. You can use the ( ) key on the calculator pad to enclose a highlighted portion of the expression in parentheses.

Relational Operators

A **relation** is a logical expression that compares two values using a relational operator. They are primarily used in conditional transformations (see "Relational and Logical Operators in Conditional Expressions" on page 81).

Logical Operators

You can use logical operators to join two relations or reverse the true/false outcome of a conditional expression. They are primarily used in conditional transformations (see "Relational and Logical Operators in Conditional Expressions" on page 81).

Functions

The function list contains over 70 built-in functions, including:

- Arithmetic functions
- Statistical functions
- Distribution functions
- Logical functions
- Date and time aggregation and extraction functions
- Missing-value functions
- Cross-case functions
- String functions

For information on specific functions, click your right mouse button on the function you want to know about or click Help in the Compute Variable dialog box.

Pasting and Editing Functions

Pasting a function into an expression. To paste a function into an expression:

1. Position the cursor in the expression at the point where you want the function to appear.

2. Double-click on the function on the Functions list (or select the function and click the ⌷▲⌷ pushbutton).

The function is inserted into the expression. If you highlight part of the expression and then insert the function, the highlighted portion of the expression is used as the first argument in the function.

Editing a function in an expression. The function is not complete until you enter the arguments, represented by question marks in the pasted function. The number of question marks indicates the minimum number of arguments required to complete the function. To edit a function:

1. Highlight the question mark(s) in the pasted function.

2. Enter the arguments. If the arguments are variable names, you can paste them from the variable list.

Conditional Expressions

You can use conditional expressions (also called logical expressions) to apply transformations to selected subsets of cases. A **conditional expression** returns a value of true, false, or missing for each case. If the result of a conditional expression is true, the transformation is applied to that case. If the result is false or missing, the transformation is not applied to the case.

To specify a conditional expression, click If... in the Compute Variable dialog box. This opens the Compute Variable If Cases dialog box, as shown in Figure 10.2.

Figure 10.2   Compute Variable If Cases dialog box

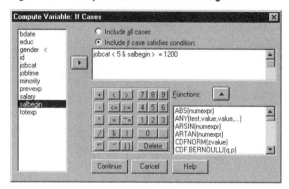

To specify a conditional expression:

1. Select Include if case satisfies condition.

2. Enter the conditional expression.

Relational and Logical Operators in Conditional Expressions

Most conditional expressions contain at least one relational operator, as in

age>=21

or

salary*3<100000

In the first example, only cases with a value of 21 or greater for *age* are selected. In the second example, *salary* multiplied by 3 must be less than 100,000 for a case to be selected.

You can also link two or more conditional expressions using logical operators, as in

age>=21 | jobcat=1

or

salary*3<100000 & jobcat~=5

In the first example, cases that meet either the *age* condition or the *jobcat* condition are selected. In the second example, both the *salary* and *jobcat* conditions must be met for a case to be selected.

Rules for Expressions

Items selected from the calculator pad, function list, and variable list are pasted in the correct format. If you type an expression in the text box or edit part of it (such as arguments for a function), remember the following simple rules:

- String variable values must be enclosed in apostrophes or quotation marks, as in **NAME='Fred'**. If the string value includes an apostrophe, enclose the string in quotation marks.

- The argument list for a function must be enclosed in parentheses. You can insert a space between the argument name and the parentheses, but none is required.

- Multiple arguments in a function must be separated by commas. You can insert spaces between arguments, but none is required.

- Each relation in a complex expression must be complete by itself. For example, **age>=18 & age<35** is correct, while **age>=18 & <35** generates an error.

- A period (.) is the only valid decimal indicator in expressions, regardless of your Windows International settings.

Additional Data Transformations

The following additional data transformations are also available on the Transform menu:

- **Count Occurrences**. Counts occurrences of the same value(s) across a list of variables within each case.

- **Rank Cases**. Computes ranks and normal and Savage scores, and classifies cases into groups based on percentile values.

- **Automatic Recode**. Recodes string and numeric variables into consecutive integers. This is useful for SPSS procedures that require integer data.

- **Create Time Series**. Creates new time series variables based on functions of existing time series variables. (Any variable measured regularly over a period of time is a time series variable.)

- **Replace Missing Values**. Replaces missing values in time series data with estimates computed with one of several methods.

11 Sorting and Selecting Data

Data files are not always organized in the ideal form for your specific needs. SPSS offers a wide range of file transformation capabilities, including the ability to:

- **Sort data**. You can sort cases based on the value of one or more variables.

- **Select subsets of cases**. You can restrict your analysis to a subset of cases or perform simultaneous analyses on different subsets.

Sorting Data

Sorting cases (sorting rows of the data file) is often useful—and sometimes necessary—for certain types of analysis. To reorder the sequence of cases in the data file based on the value of one or more sorting variables, from the menus choose:

Data
  Sort Cases...

This opens the Sort Cases dialog box, as shown in Figure 11.1.

Figure 11.1   Sort Cases dialog box

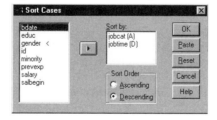

If you select multiple sort variables, the order in which they appear on the Sort by list determines the order in which cases are sorted. For example, based on the Sort by list in Figure 11.1, cases will be sorted by descending value of *job-*

time within ascending categories of *jobcat.* For string variables, uppercase letters precede their lowercase counterparts in sort order (for example, the string value "Yes" comes before "yes" in sort order).

Split-File Processing

To split your data file into separate groups for analysis, from the menus choose:

Data
  Split File...

This opens the Split File dialog box, as shown in Figure 11.2.

The Split File procedure automatically sorts the data file based on the values of the grouping variables. If the original order of cases is important, do not save the file after using the Split File option.

Figure 11.2   Split File dialog box

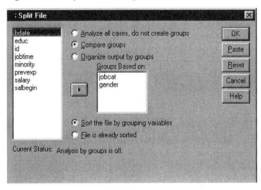

To split the data file into separate groups for analysis:

1. Select Compare groups or Organize output by groups.

2. Select the variable(s) to use to split the file into separate groups.

You can use numeric, short string, and long string variables as grouping variables. A separate analysis is performed for each subgroup defined by the grouping variables. If you select multiple grouping variables, the order in which they appear on the Groups Based on list determines the manner in which cases are grouped. For example, based on the Groups Based on list in Figure 11.2, cases will be grouped by the value of *gender* within categories of *jobcat.*

Sorting Cases for Split-File Processing

The Split File procedure creates a new subgroup each time it encounters a different value for one of the grouping variables. Therefore, it is important to sort cases based on the values of the grouping variables before invoking split-file processing.

By default, Split File automatically sorts the data file based on the values of the grouping variables. If the file is already sorted in the proper order, you can save processing time if you select File is already sorted.

Turning Split-File Processing On and Off

You can easily reopen the Split File dialog box by clicking on

Once you invoke split-file processing, it remains in effect for the rest of the session unless you turn it off.

- Analyze all cases. Turns split-file processing off.
- Compare groups and Organize output by groups. Turns split-file processing on.

If split-file processing is in effect, the message Split File on appears on the status bar at the bottom of the SPSS application window.

Selecting Subsets of Cases

You can restrict your analysis to a specific subgroup based on criteria that include variables and complex expressions. You can also select a random sample of cases. The criteria used to define a subgroup can include:

- Variable values and ranges
- Date and time ranges
- Case (row) numbers
- Arithmetic expressions
- Logical expressions
- Functions

To select a subset of cases for analysis, from the menus choose:

Data
  Select Cases...

This opens the Select Cases dialog box, as shown in Figure 11.3.

Figure 11.3   Select Cases dialog box

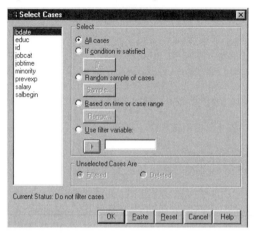

Unselected Cases

If you delete unselected cases and save the file, the cases cannot be recovered.

You can choose one of the following alternatives for the treatment of unselected cases:

- **Filtered**. Unselected cases are not included in the analysis but remain in the data file. You can use the unselected cases later in the session if you turn filtering off. If you select a random sample or if you select cases based on a conditional expression, this generates a variable named *filter_$* with a value of 1 for selected cases and a value of 0 for unselected cases.

- **Deleted**. Unselected cases are deleted from the data file. By reducing the number of cases in the open data file, you can save processing time. Deleted cases can be recovered only by exiting from the file without saving any changes and then reopening the file. The deletion of cases is permanent if you save the changes to the data file.

Selecting Cases Based on Conditional Expressions

To select cases based on a conditional expression, select **If condition is satisfied** and click **If...** in the Select Cases dialog box. This opens the Select Cases If dialog box, as shown in Figure 11.4.

Figure 11.4   Select Cases If dialog box

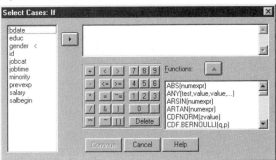

The conditional expression can use existing variable names, constants, arithmetic operators, logical operators, relational operators, and functions. You can type and edit the expression in the text box just like text in a output window (see Chapter 4). You can also use the calculator pad, variable list, and function list to paste elements into the expression. See Chapter 10 for more information on working with conditional expressions.

Selecting a Random Sample

To obtain a random sample, select Random sample of cases in the Select Cases dialog box and click Sample.... This opens the Select Cases Random Sample dialog box, as shown in Figure 11.5.

Figure 11.5   Select Cases Random Sample dialog box

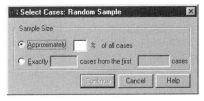

Sample Size. You can select one of the following alternatives for sample size:

- **Approximately**. A user-specified percentage. SPSS generates a random sample of approximately the specified percentage of cases.

- **Exactly**. A user-specified number of cases. You must also specify the number of cases from which to generate the sample. This second number should be less than or equal to the total number of cases in the data file. If the number exceeds the total number of cases in the data file, the sample will contain proportionally fewer cases than the requested number.

Selecting a Time Range or Case Range

To select a range of cases based on dates, times, or observation (row) number, select Based on time or case range and click Range... in the Select Cases dialog box. This opens the Select Cases Range dialog box, as shown on the left in Figure 11.6. For time series data with defined date variables, you can select a range of dates and/or times based on the defined date variables, as shown on the right in Figure 11.6. For other data files, you can select a range of observation (row) numbers. To generate date variables for time series data, use the Define Dates option on the Data menu.

Figure 11.6   Select Cases Range dialog boxes

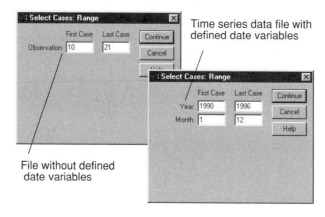

Time series data file with defined date variables

File without defined date variables

In a time series data file, each case represents observations at a different time, and the file is sorted in chronological order. To define date variables for time series data, use the Define Dates option on the Data menu.

First Case. Enter the starting date and/or time values for the range. If no date variables are defined, enter the starting observation number (row number in the Data Editor, unless Split File is on). If you do not specify a Last Case value, all cases from the starting date/time to the end of the time series are selected.

Last Case. Enter the ending date and/or time values for the range. If no date variables are defined, enter the ending observation number (row number in the Data Editor, unless Split File is on). If you do not specify a First Case value, all cases from the beginning of the time series up to the ending date/time are selected.

Case Selection Status

If you have selected a subset of cases but have not discarded unselected cases, unselected cases are marked in the Data Editor with a diagonal line through the row number, as shown in Figure 11.7.

Figure 11.7   Case selection status

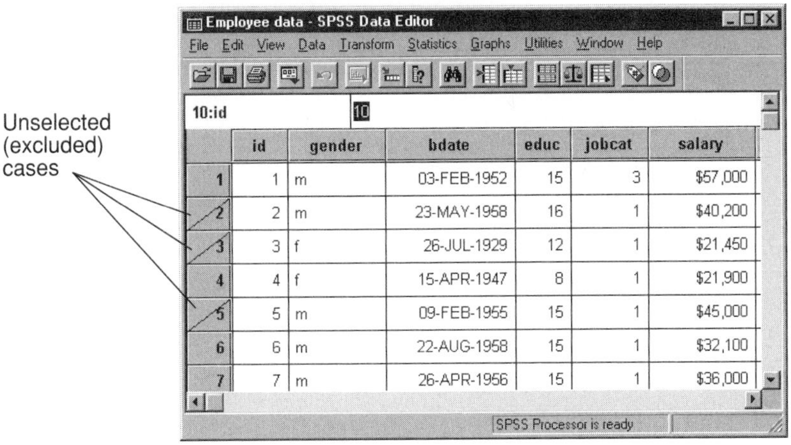

Unselected (excluded) cases

12 Additional Statistical Procedures

This chapter contains brief tutorials for selected statistical procedures. It also refers to other chapters in this manual where other procedures are shown. The procedures are grouped according to the order in which they appear on the Statistics menu.

The examples are designed to illustrate sample specifications required to run a statistical procedure. Most of the examples use the *Employee data.sav* file, which is described in Chapter 4. The exponential smoothing example uses the *Inventor.sav* file, which contains inventory data collected over a period of 70 days. In the examples in this chapter, you must run the procedures to see the output.

For information about individual items in a dialog box, click Help. If you want to locate a specific statistic, such as percentiles, use the Search facility in the Help system, which is described in Chapter 2. For additional information about interpreting the results obtained by running these procedures, consult a statistics or data analysis textbook.

Summarizing Data

The Summarize submenu on the Statistics menu provides techniques for summarizing data with statistics and charts. The following are brief tutorials for the Frequencies and Explore procedures.

Frequencies

An example showing a frequency table and a bar chart is provided in Chapter 1. In that example, the Frequencies procedure was used to analyze the variable *jobcat*, which has a small number of distinct job categories. If the variable you want to analyze has a large number of different values, you can use the Frequencies procedure to generate summary statistics and a histogram. A **histogram** is a chart that shows the number of cases in each of several groups. To generate sta-

tistics and a histogram of the current salaries in the *Employee data.sav* file, fol-
low these steps:

❶ From the menus choose:

Statistics
  Summarize ▶
    Frequencies...

This opens the Frequencies dialog box, as shown in Figure 12.1.

Figure 12.1   Frequencies dialog box

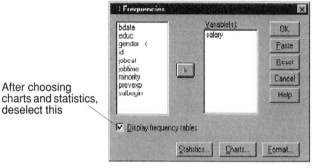

After choosing
charts and statistics,
deselect this

❷ Select *salary* as a variable.

❸ Click Charts... to open the Frequencies Charts dialog box, as shown in Figure
12.2.

Figure 12.2   Frequencies Charts dialog box

❹ Select Histograms and With normal curve, and then click Continue.

⑤ To select summary statistics, click Statistics... in the Frequencies dialog box. Select Mean, Std. deviation, and Maximum in the Frequencies Statistics dialog box, and then click Continue.

⑥ Deselect Display frequency tables in the main Frequencies dialog box.

(If you leave this item selected and display a frequency table for current salary, the output shows an entry for every distinct value of salary, making a very long table.)

⑦ Click OK to run the procedure.

The Output Navigator shows the requested statistics and chart. Each bar in the histogram represents the number of employees within a salary range, and the salary values displayed are the range midpoints. As requested, a normal curve is superimposed on the chart.

Explore

Suppose you want to look further at the distribution of salary for each job category in the *Employee data.sav* file. With the Explore procedure, you can examine the distribution of salary within categories of another variable.

❶ From the menus choose:

Statistics
  Summarize ▶
    Explore...

This opens the Explore dialog box, as shown in Figure 12.3.

Figure 12.3   Explore dialog box

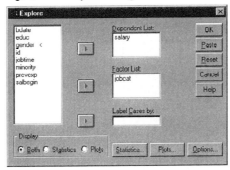

❷ Select *salary* for the Dependent List.

❸ Select *jobcat* for the Factor List.

④ Click OK to run the Explore procedure.

In the output, descriptive statistics and a stem-and-leaf plot are displayed for the current salaries in each job category. The Output Navigator also contains a boxplot comparing the salaries in the job categories. For each category, the boxplot shows the median, interquartile range (25th to 75th percentile), outliers (indicated by O), and extreme values (indicated by *).

More about Summarizing Data

There are many ways to summarize data in SPSS. For example, to calculate medians or percentiles, use the Frequencies procedure or the Explore procedure. The following lists some additional methods:

- **Descriptives.** For current salary, you can calculate standard scores, sometimes called **Z scores**. Use the Descriptives procedure and select Save standardized values as variables.

- **Crosstabs.** Instead of making one table, as in the example of the Crosstabs procedure in Chapter 4, you can create separate tables for males and females by moving *gender* into the layer box and selecting *minority* as the column variable.

- **List Cases.** You can use the List Cases procedure to write to your output window a listing of the actual values of gender, job category, and current salary of the first 25 or 50 employees.

Comparing Means

The Compare Means submenu on the Statistics menu provides techniques for displaying descriptive statistics and testing whether differences are significant between two means for both independent and paired samples. You can also test whether differences are significant among more than two independent means by using the One-Way ANOVA procedure. The following tutorials use two procedures from this group, Means and Paired-Samples T Test.

Means

In the employee data file, several variables are available for dividing the employees into groups. You can then calculate various statistics in order to compare the groups. For example, you can compute the average (mean) salaries for minority and non-minority males and females. To calculate the means, use the following steps:

❶ From the menus choose:

Statistics
    Compare Means ▶
        Means...

This opens the Means dialog box, as shown in Figure 12.4.

Figure 12.4   Means dialog box (layer 1)

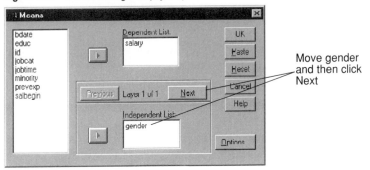

Move gender
and then click
Next

❷ Select *salary* for the Dependent List.

❸ Select *gender* for the Independent List in layer 1.

❹ Click Next. This creates another layer, as shown in Figure 12.5.

Figure 12.5   Means dialog box (layer 2)

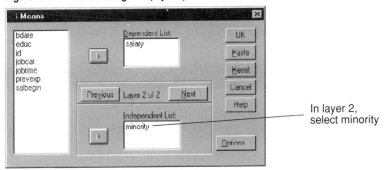

In layer 2,
select minority

❺ Select *minority* for the Independent List in layer 2.

❻ Click OK to run the procedure.

Paired-Samples T Test

When the data are structured in such a way that there are two observations on the same individual or observations that are matched by another variable on two individuals (twins, for example), the samples are paired. In the employee data file, a beginning salary and a current salary are listed for each employee. If the company is prospering, periodic raises would probably be granted, and you would certainly expect that the average current salary is greater than the average beginning salary.

To carry out a *t* test of the beginning salary and current salary means, use the following steps:

❶ From the menus choose:

Statistics
  Compare Means ▶
    Paired-Samples T Test...

This opens the Paired-Samples T Test dialog box, as shown in Figure 12.6.

Figure 12.6   Paired-Samples T Test dialog box

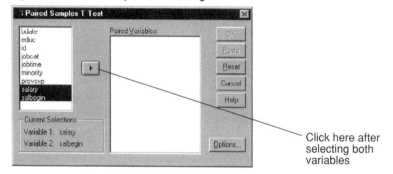

❷ Click *salary*. The variable is displayed in the Current Selections group.

❸ Click *salbegin*. The variable is displayed in the Current Selections group.

❹ Click ▶ to move the pair to the Paired Variables list.

❺ Click OK to run the procedure.

The results, as expected, show that the current salary is significantly different from the beginning salary, as indicated by the small probability displayed in the *Sig. (2-tailed)* column. The data structure in this example is similar to an experiment in which the same person is observed before and after an intervention.

More about Comparing Means

The following examples suggest some ways in which you can use other procedures to compare means.

- **Independent-Samples T Test.** When you use a *t* test to compare means of one variable across independent groups, the samples are independent. Males and females in the employee file can be divided into independent groups by the variable *gender*. You can use a *t* test to determine if the mean current salaries of males and females are the same.

- **One-Sample T Test.** You can test whether the average salary of clerical workers in this company differs from a national or state average. Use Select Cases... on the Data menu to select the cases with *jobcat*=1. Then, run the One-Sample T Test procedure to compare *salary* and the test value 35000.

- **One-Way ANOVA.** The variable *jobcat* divides employees into three independent groups by employment category. You can use the One-Way ANOVA procedure to test whether mean beginning salaries for the three groups are significantly different.

ANOVA Models

The General Linear Models submenu on the Statistics menu provides techniques for testing univariate analysis-of-variance models. (If you have only one factor, you can use the One-Way ANOVA procedure on the Compare Means submenu.)

Simple Factorial ANOVA

The Simple Factorial ANOVA procedure performs an analysis of variance for factorial designs.

In this example, you will need to recode the string variable *gender* into a numeric variable before you can run the procedure.

① From the menus choose:

Transform
  Automatic Recode...

This opens the Automatic Recode dialog box, as shown in Figure 12.7.

Figure 12.7   Automatic Recode dialog box

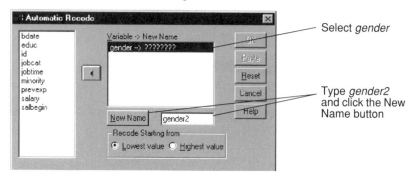

Select *gender*

Type *gender2* and click the New Name button

❷ Select the variable *gender* and move it into the Variable -> New Name list.

❸ Type *gender2* in the New Name text box, then click the **New Name** button.

❹ Click OK to run the procedure.

This creates a new numeric variable called **gender2,** which has a value of 1 for females and a value of 2 for males. Now a simple factorial design can be used to test if employees with differing race and gender classifications have the same beginning salaries.

❶ From the menus choose:

Statistics
  General Linear Model ▶
    Simple Factorial...

This opens the Simple Factorial ANOVA dialog box, as shown on the left in Figure 12.8.

Figure 12.8   Simple Factorial ANOVA dialog box

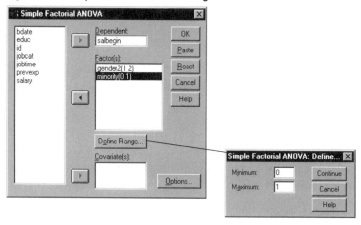

❷ Select *salbegin* as the dependent variable.

❸ Select *gender2* and *minority* as factors.

❹ With *minority* selected, click Define Range....

This opens the Define Range dialog box, as shown on the right in Figure 12.8.

❺ Type **0** in the Minimum text box and **1** in the Maximum text box. Then click Continue.

❻ With *gender2* selected, click Define Range....

❼ Type **1** in the Minimum text box and **2** in the Maximum text box. Then click Continue.

For *gender*, the value 2 is the code for male and the value 1 is the code for female. For *minority*, the value 0 is the code for white and the value 1 is the code for minority.

In any dialog box, you can click the right mouse button on any variable to pop up information about that variable.

Hint: If you do not know the range for a variable, click on it with the *right* mouse button to pop up a variable information window. (To do this, you will temporarily need to cancel the Define Range dialog box.)

❽ Click OK to run the procedure.

In the output, you can see that the effects of *gender2* and *minority* are definitely significant and that the observed significance level of the interaction of *gender2* and *minority* is 0.11. For further interpretation, consult a statistics or data analysis textbook.

Correlating Variables

The Correlate submenu on the Statistics menu provides measures of association for two or more numeric variables. Following are an example of the Bivariate Correlation procedure and a brief tutorial using the Partial Correlations procedure.

Bivariate Correlations

You can calculate a Pearson correlation coefficient to see if there is a linear association between *salary* (current salary) and *salbegin* (beginning salary).

Partial Correlations

The Partial Correlations procedure calculates partial correlation coefficients that describe the relationship between two variables while adjusting for the effects of one or more additional variables.

You can estimate the correlation between *salbegin* and *salary*, controlling for the linear effects of *jobtime* (time on the job) and *prevexp* (previous experience). The number of control variables determines the order of the partial correlation coefficient.

① From the menus choose:

Statistics
  Correlate ▶
    Partial...

This opens the Partial Correlations dialog box, as shown in Figure 12.9.

Figure 12.9   Partial Correlations dialog box

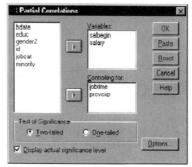

② Select *salbegin* and *salary* as variables.

③ Select *jobtime* and *prevexp* as control variables.

④ Click OK to run the procedure.

The output shows a table of partial correlation coefficients, the number of cases, and the significance level for the pair *salary* and *salbegin*.

Regression Analysis

The Regression submenu on the Statistics menu provides regression techniques, including curve estimation. Following is a brief tutorial using the Linear Regression procedure.

Linear Regression

The Linear Regression procedure examines the relationship between a dependent variable and a set of independent variables. You can use it to predict an employee's current salary (the dependent variable) from independent variables such as number of years of education, months of experience, gender, and minority.

❶ From the menus choose:

Statistics
  Regression ▶
    Linear...

This opens the Linear Regression dialog box, as shown in Figure 12.10.

Figure 12.10 Linear Regression dialog box

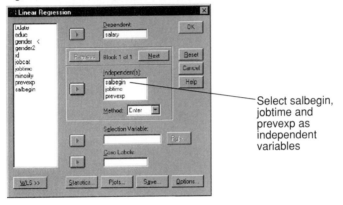

Select salbegin, jobtime and prevexp as independent variables

❷ Select *salary* as the dependent variable.

❸ Select *salbegin*, *jobtime*, and *prevexp* as the independent variables.

❹ Click OK to run the procedure.

The output contains goodness-of-fit statistics and the coefficients for the variables. By examining the significance column, you can see that *jobtime* should not be in the equation.

Examining fit. To see how well the regression model fits your data, you can examine the residuals and other types of diagnostics that this procedure provides. In the Linear Regression dialog box, click Save... to see a list of the new variables you can add to your data file. If you generate any of these variables, they will not be available in a later SPSS session unless you save the data file.

Methods. If you have collected a large number of independent variables and want to build a regression model that includes only variables that are statistically related to the dependent variable, you can select a method from the drop-down list. For example, if you select Stepwise in the above example, only variables that meet the criteria in the Linear Regression Options dialog box are entered in the equation.

More about Regression Procedures

The following example uses another regression procedure:

- **Curve Estimation.** You can use the Curve Estimation procedure to fit linear, quadratic, and cubic models of *salary* as a function of *salbegin*.

To use the Curve Estimation procedure for predictions for time series data, in the Independent group, select Time and then click Save.... Select Predicted values and Predict through. Make entries in the Curve Estimation Save dialog box similar to the entries described for prediction in "Exponential Smoothing" on p. 103.

Nonparametric Tests

The Nonparametric Tests submenu on the Statistics menu provides nonparametric tests for one sample or for two or more paired or independent samples. Nonparametric tests do not require assumptions about the shape of the distributions from which the data originate. Following is a brief tutorial using the Chi-Square Test procedure.

Chi-Square

The Chi-Square Test procedure is used to test hypotheses about the relative proportion of cases falling into several mutually exclusive groups. You can test the hypothesis that employees in the company occur in the same proportions of gender as the general population (50% males, 50% females).

If you have not done so already, you will need to recode the string variable *gender* into a numeric variable called *gender2*. This process is described in "Simple Factorial ANOVA" on p. 97.

❶ From the menus choose:

Statistics
  Nonparametric Tests ▶
    Chi-Square...

This opens the Chi-Square Test dialog box, as shown in Figure 12.11.

Figure 12.11 Chi-Square Test dialog box

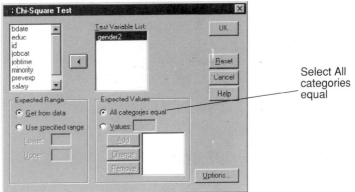

Select All
categories
equal

② Select *gender2* as the test variable.

③ Click Values in the Expected Values group.

④ Select All categories equal.

⑤ Click OK to run the procedure.

The output shows a table of the expected and residual values for the categories. The chi-square test shows a significant difference.

Time Series Analysis

A **time series variable** is a variable whose values are recorded at regular intervals over a period of time. The Time Series submenu on the Statistics menu provides exponential smoothing that can be used for predictions. Following is a brief tutorial using the Exponential Smoothing procedure.

Exponential Smoothing

The Exponential Smoothing procedure performs exponential smoothing of time series data. It creates new series containing predicted values and residuals.

For example, you can fit a model for inventory data and use it to predict the next week's inventory. Suppose that for 70 days you have kept track of the inventory of power supplies and that you want to construct a model and then use it to forecast power supplies for the next week.

① Open the *Inventor.sav* file. (It is in the directory where SPSS is installed.)

❷ From the menus choose:

Statistics
  Time Series ▶
    Exponential Smoothing...

This opens the Exponential Smoothing dialog box, as shown in Figure 12.12.

Figure 12.12 Exponential Smoothing dialog box

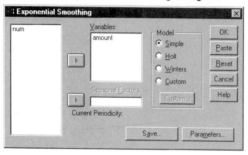

❸ Select *amount* for the Variables list.

❹ Click Parameters... to specify the procedure.

This opens the Exponential Smoothing Parameters dialog box, as shown in Figure 12.13.

Figure 12.13 Exponential Smoothing Parameters dialog box

Click here

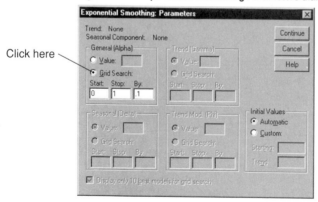

❺ To search for the best general parameter, click Grid Search and then click Continue.

❻ To create a new variable that contains predicted values, click Save....

This opens the Exponential Smoothing Save dialog box, as shown in Figure 12.14.

Figure 12.14 Exponential Smoothing Save dialog box

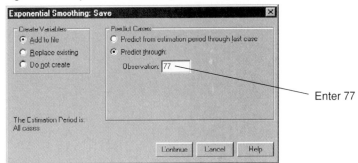

⑦ Click Predict through and type **77** in the Observation text box.

This adds 7 days to the original 70.

⑧ Click Continue and then in the main dialog box, click OK.

This runs the procedure and adds new variables *fit_1* and *err_1*. The variable *fit_1* contains the fitted values and the seven new predicted values. The variable *err_1* contains residual values for the original 70 cases; you can use the residuals for further analysis. If you want to save the new variables, select Save As... from the File menu and save the data file under a new name.

⑨ To see a chart of the original data and the new fit line, from the menus choose:

Graphs
  Sequence...

This opens the Sequence Charts dialog box, as shown in Figure 12.15.

Figure 12.15 Sequence Charts dialog box

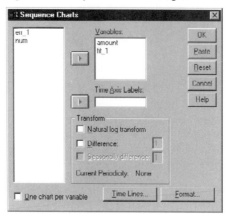

⑩ Select *amount* and *fit_1* as variables.

⑪ Click OK to run the procedure.

The resulting chart shows both the actual number of power supplies and the fit line plotted on the same axes. The predicted values are plotted for the next week at the right side of the chart.

Index